HOW TO WRITE A BETTER ANYTHING

HOW TO WRITE A BETTER ANYTHING

THE CREATIVE WRITER'S HANDBOOK

Dorothy Farmiloe

Black Moss Press

Published by Black Moss Press, P.O. Box 143, Station A, Windsor, Ontario. Financial assistance towards the publication of this book was provided by the Ontario Arts Council and the Canada Council.

Black Moss Press books are distributed in Canada and the U.S. by Firefly Books, 2 Essex Avenue, Unit #5, Thornhill, Ontario. All orders should be directed there.

Designed by Tim Inkster, printed and bound by The Porcupine's Quill (Erin) in October of 1979. The stock is Zephyr Antique Laid and the type is Garamond.

ISBN 0-88753-058-3

CONTENTS

CONTENTS

INTRODUCTION

One definition of poetry — and it applies to fine writing of all kinds — includes the experience or truth the work contains, a reaction to that experience, and the craftsmanship that shapes the first two into a work of art. Since your experience can come from just about anywhere on earth — or under or above it for that matter — and the emotional reaction triggers itself off, it is in the area of craftsmanship that a how-to book will be helpful. For whatever else a piece of good writing is, it is a crafted object. Your original thought in untouched words is the raw material, you are the craftsman.

Just what does craftsmanship imply, anyway? It used to mean long years of training apprenticed to a master. All artists, from cabinet makers to portrait painters, used to go this route. They would begin by learning the rudiments of their trade as Michelangelo began by learning as a child to mix paints for his teacher before ever being allowed to hold a brush much less paint a Sistine Chapel. Most artists today, striving for individuality, tend to spurn the traditional apprenticeship method because they believe working too close to another artist can adversely affect their style. They prefer to do their own thing right from the start. Which is all right up to a point, but whereas there is something to be said for the primitive Grandma Moses style of painting, there is not much to be said for writing that betrays lack of knowledge in the basics of language. For one thing, editors aren't interested in manuscripts that show evidence of sloppy grammar and spelling. Keep it simple but keep it literate.

A feeling for grammar can be developed in much the same way

as an ear for music. Some grammar sense will be absorbed by osmosis if you read and analyze the work of other writers. In a recent interview, Farley Mowat, who says he knows nothing of grammar but has always done a tremendous amount of reading, advises doing two things to become a writer: to practice as a reader and a writer. Read. Read. Read. I hope you will be tempted to follow up on some of the published writers mentioned in the following chapters, will make an effort to get their books and read them in depth. If you have a particular writer you admire above all others, read everything of his or hers you can get your hands on. Don't worry about sounding too much like your acknowledged master. You will develop your own style as you grow and eventually the early influences will disappear.

To a true craftsman, theory is as important as technique. When Michelangelo started sculpturing he realized he had to know what lay beneath the covering of human skin, but there were no anatomy books to guide him. So he stole into a vault night after night to dissect corpses knowing that if he got caught he faced the death penalty for violating a dead body. Fortunately, we aren't all called on to exhibit such harrowing dedication to our art, but we do have to know what lies beneath the skin and why things move as they do.

Because an understanding of the principles behind good writing will help you get beyond the apprenticeship stage faster, existing theories are examined and illustrated for you in the following pages. If I seem to quote poetry for illustration more often than prose, it is for two reasons: first, a short poem is complete in itself and any point being made can be seen in full context; second, poetry more than any other form of writing necessitates precision of language. Any of the devices used by poets — imagery is the prime example — can be used to good effect by all writers. The following chapters illustrate the universality of these devices by drawing together examples from different kinds of media. Where the title of a work is mentioned without a quoted passage, it is to get you to look up the work yourself and assess the principles involved.

As far as theory in writing goes, the principles that govern it are extremely flexible. Every so-called rule outlined for you in this handbook can be — and has been — broken by some writer somewhere for some purpose or other. That is part of the definition of creative writing. But before you can break the rules creatively you have to know what they are. Then you can twist them into any exception you please. All artists who break new ground have to work out their own guiding principles eventually.

You learn to write by writing. All the advice in the world won't help if you only read about it. You have to put theory into practice and get down to work on a more or less regular basis. Most successful writers have a definite time and place for writing. If your name is Farley Mowat and you make your living from your books, you can afford a separate retreat away from the house and can threaten dire consequences to anyone who interrupts you while you are there. Most writers aren't this fortunate as far as space goes, but we can all find a quiet corner somewhere. I know a writer who sets up his typewriter in the dining room after the children are in bed; another who gets up at five every morning and works at the kitchen table; a woman who writes in the family car in a supermarket parking lot. If you really want to write, you will find the time and the place.

Dan Ross is another Canadian writer who makes his living with his typewriter. He is, in fact, the most prolific novelist in North America with over 270 romances to his credit — and he didn't start writing them until he was fifty years old. Every day, with his dictionary and a book of quotations, he goes down to the furnace room and writes.

Another thing. When inspiration — or whatever you want to call the inception of an original idea — grips you, don't let it escape. It is a good idea to carry a notebook and pen with you at all times. I used to keep a flashlight and a notepad on the floor by the bed so that I could catch those fleeting late-night thoughts without putting on the light and waking my sleeping spouse. Other writers, especially those who do a lot of driving, use a tape-recorder. However you do it, record your thoughts right away. You can knock them into shape later when you are set up in your own nook with an old jamjar full of pens and pencils and a notebook full of ideas. Then you can get on with mastering craft.

Craftsmanship in writing means intimate knowledge and control of all the tools that can be used to shape thought into art. Dylan Thomas, from whom Bob Dylan took his stage name, said that he treated words as a craftsman does his wood or stone or what-have-you, to hew, carve, mold, coil, polish and plane them into patterns, sequences, sculptures, figures of sound expressing some lyrical impulse, some spiritual doubt or conviction, some dimly realized truth that he had to try to reach or realize. In spite of his rich gift of gab, Thomas was a word-polisher who finished his work with the discriminating eye of an artist. You could do worse than keep Thomas' definition of a craftsman in mind.

Once you reach the point of getting your thoughts out, either by writing them down or talking them into a tape-recorder, you have taken the first step in the working process of becoming a writer. Whether you remain a weekend wordbutcher or become a master craftsman has much to do with how you use the tools of the writer's trade, from simple words to more complex forms of expression. You may believe, passionately, that creativity is a mysterious God-given gift or you may feel it is merely an urge that results from much reading that has fueled your own imagination. Or you may simply have something to say and want to say it well. Whatever your motive for writing, the following chapters can help you once you get something down on paper.

WORDS AND THE
DISCRIMINATING
WRITER

It is words, individually and together, that carry the weight of what the writer says, and since you want to improve, the place to start is with these important little posties of communication. Depending on what you want to say and how you want to say it, your words can be matter-of-fact or emotional, gramatically correct or slangy, usual or unusual. Craftsmanship in writing does not necessarily demand a fund of intricate expressions or a vocabulary stuffed like a dictionary. What you need to express your thoughts are the most suitable words and these can often be very simple ones.

Keeping it simple, however, need not mean using dull language. A tremendous range of words exists to lift your efforts out of the pedestrian class and into the untested blue. When it comes to flying with words, a Piper Cub can be just as exciting as a Boeing 747 since it is not the size of the words but what you do with them that counts. In *Power Politics*, in what is probably the most devastating love poetry ever written, Margaret Atwood uses short familiar words to perform verbal aerobatics with stunning virtuosity. In the now-famous prologue poem "You fit into me," a hook-and-eye image is twisted into a fish hook and an open eye. There are no big words in the poem at all.

The English language has so many levels of expression, and so much variety within each level, that you have too wide a choice of words to start with. Some picking and choosing is necessary. Select your words the way a painter selects the colors for a painting. Before a painter begins, he decides which colors will give him the effect he is after and he then puts only these on his palette, ignoring the others.

This is the kind of discriminating eye you want when choosing words for your word-palette. The technical term for verbal discrimination is diction.

DICTION IS THE CHOICE OF WORDS, SELECTED FROM ONE AREA OF LANGUAGE, THAT A WRITER USES IN A SECTION OF WORK.

In her novel *The Edible Woman*, Margaret Atwood shows the same precision of word-choice she displays in her poetry. Much of the description in *The Edible Woman*, whose theme concerns vulnerability to having one's personality "eaten" (absorbed) by another's, is drawn from areas having to do with food. Near the end of the story, the heroine bakes a cake in the shape of a woman. The ingredients are itemized: eggs, flour, sugar, and so on. Everything in the novel is connected, from diction and images to theme and title.

Diction can be defined in another way as a family of words — that is, all the members are related. A word that has no connection with the others, or that calls up the wrong connotations, can spoil the total effect.

Moments like these
when i catch you
            i'm caught
myself
by the mood

today it is the sun
about your frame
as you bend and read

it is soap-opera mellow
this blend and flood
of emotions i have

your image
a prism
rainbow colors across
this silent second

i want to cross over
to you
        and won't
not wanting you
to know
i've added the
memory of this
moment
to my life

Linda Renwick

In this poem, "frame" in the second stanza is an angular word which sits awkwardly among the others. Change it to "body" and you not only have a softer image, you have an alliteration of *b* sounds:

today it is the sun
about your body
as you bend and read . . . .

"Frame" is the kind of word Dickens might have selected for the following passage from *Hard Times* where the diction is related to a stark unadorned classroom where only the bare facts were taught:

The scene was a plain, bare, monotonous vault of a schoolroom, and the speaker's square forefinger emphasized his observations by underscoring every sentence with a line on the schoolmaster's sleeve. The emphasis was helped by the speaker's square wall of a forehead, which had his eyebrows for its base, while his eyes found commodious cellarage in two dark caves, overshadowed by the wall.

If Dickens had used adjectives descriptive of the usual kind of schoolroom where the walls are decorated with gaily coloured pictures drawn by the children, it would have greatly lessened the impact of his message. He was protesting his society's utilitarian philosophy which was unrelieved by the saving graces of imagination. So the diction in his paragraph is chosen from a severe utilitarian family — plain, bare, monotonous, and so on. All the words in the paragraph work together to give us a picture of a monotonous speaker. But the *writing* is not monotonous.

Concrete versus Abstract

Nouns and adjectives in particular need to be precise if they are to carry the meaning you intend them to. Suppose you are writing a novel and you want to tell the reader that the heroine is very beautiful. You can say it in just those words, but "beautiful," besides being overused, is an abstraction that does not give a clear picture by itself. If you compare the girl to a well-known beauty, however, your words will form a visual impression for the reader. The Egyptian queen Nefertiti was one of the most exquisitely lovely women of all antiquity if we can credit the likeness of her in the Berlin Museum. So you might say your heroine was "as beautiful as Nefertiti." Better yet, you can avoid the adjective altogether with "She wore her hair swept up off her face which emphasized her Nefertiti-like features." There you have it with concrete details instead of an abstract word.

Abstractions or generalities weaken any description. The discriminating writer rejects them altogether and chooses words that give the reader something he can see, feel, hear, smell or taste. Abstract words should be avoided for another reason: they give the reader nothing beyond the context in which they are used and frequently little even there. Try to define happiness without your own personal interpretation. The word has such different meanings, depending on whose happiness is at stake, that is has no substance in a phrase like "life, liberty and the pursuit of happiness." But when the general term is appended with an object, "happiness is a warm puppy," then you have something the mind can grasp and hold onto, an image that remains on the retina of the inner eye. (Images are explored more fully in Chapter Four.)

Strong Verbs

Pictorial description is only one aspect of creative writing and a somewhat static one at that. You also want your work to move. Plot formations aside for the moment, there are other, more subtle, ways of moving a play, short story or novel ahead. The most dramatic action words are verbs. In a good drama, strong verbs reinforce the action and help carry the play forward. Shakespeare, the greatest wordsmith who ever lived, knew this. Under his pen whole sentences of meaning were condensed into a few action words. Macbeth speaks of "*vaulting* ambition which *o'erleaps* itself." In Hamlet, one of the guards in the first act complains, "The air *bites* shrewdly. It is very cold." And in *Lear*, the old man howls, "Blow, winds, and *crack* your cheeks. Rage! Blow!"

Get directly to the matter at hand by using single strong verb.

forms. Note that Shakespeare doesn't drag the verb out with "The air is biting." The shorter "bites" has more punch. (Use the present tense instead of the present progressive.) Speaking of punch, listen sometime to the way a sports announcer matches his words to the action he is describing. A boxer doesn't just hit — he slashes, jabs, punches, pounds, lands a swift uppercut or a haymaker. In an account of a ballgame, the sportscaster never says, "The ball was just hit into centre field by Aaron." He says, "Aaron just slammed one into centre field." Use strong verbs and get them up front where the action is. (Use the active voice instead of the passive.)

Special Effects
The words in a paragraph or poem, since they belong to a family of diction, should reveal a connection with each other, but if they are too closely related they can be as boring as an uncle who tells the same story over and over. Frequently, a stunningly different word can cause a line to come alive, rather like introducing an unconventional Aunt Mame to the rest of the family. Words can be so intoxicating that some writers go beyond the range of words available and come up with made-up or fantasy words of their own, words you won't find in any dictionary. A familiar example of this is the nonsense vocabulary devised by Lewis Carroll for his poem "Jabberwocky."

> 'Twas brillig and the slithy toves
>   Did gyre and gimble in the wabe
> All mimsy were the borogroves
>   And the mome raths outgrabe.

These peculiar words don't mean much and aren't intended to. Occasionally, though, a poet will devise new words or combine familiar ones in an original way so that they acquire richer meaning. The next poem is full of lovely surprises. Note how the poet has turned the words "paunch," "parliament," and "psycho" — words normally used as nouns — into verbs. Note, too, the use of slang and colloquialisms. Much of the appeal of this poem is in its fresh use of language.

Senators love us, Clarie, monkey,
Love us criminals, their soul food,
Ambition food, whimsy food.
Didn't she ride a donkey?

She'd no ring neither, Clarie,
Mary'd got no ring.
And Jesus a wee thing.
I've made him a donkey, Clarie,

Made, made my kid a donkey,
Stuffed my spended life into the seam.
Senator saw me paunch out the dream.
Nice, she smiled, — Clarie, Sweet Mary

Hold my gut straight to time
Nor let the devil sear my skull wall.
For love of a kiss on the Mall
I'll be in church come Sunday chime.

They've been. They've talked. They've gone.
Lawyer-bosses. Newsmen. Doctors.
Parliament gung-ho's. Senators.
Parliamented and psyched and gone.

Josephine Hambleton Tessier

As a class, the poets are probably more experimental with language than other writers are, but you don't have to be a poet to use words poetically. Lois Wilson, the editor of *Chatelaine's Gardening Book*, has turned a basic reference volume into delightful reading where vines are "gay gymnasts" and flowers "butterflies." No matter what you are writing — a treatise on gardening, a children's story, a poem — let your words sing and soar and they will carry the reader with them.

Dictionaries
How curious are you about words? Not long ago, while looking up another word in the dictionary, I came across "squamous." Squamous??? What an odd word. It seemed to have a poem

embedded in it much the same as marble already has a statue in it —
according to some sculptors — waiting to be freed. Here is the poem:

a scaly little monster of a word
uncovered hiding in the dictionary
next to squalor squirms for
recognition
   write a poem using
   squamous   done

forms locked in an elephant's bones
until Henry Moore released them

Dictionaries are as indispensible to a writer as his typewriter. They
are also exciting to a word freak. (Were you curious enough to look
up squamous?) It goes without saying that if you have any doubt
about the meaning or spelling of a word, look it up. I keep the Gage
Dictionary of Canadian English, Senior Dictionary, on my desk
beside *Roget's International Thesaurus*. If you depend on a
thesaurus, you still have to be discriminating enough to choose the
most suitable word. Look up "intestines" in a thesaurus and you will
find a list of words with these among them: entrails, insides, innards,
vitals, guts, abdomen. In the fourth stanza of the poem, "From
Millhaven," if the author had used any of these except "gut" the
effect would not have been the same. The other words don't have the
same shade of meaning. You will probably find a thesaurus helpful at
times although it is no substitute for imagination.

Summary
As a writer, then, you have an exciting range of words available from
which to choose. You may select any you please, even to the extent of
making up your own, as long as they fit the meaning. Do develop a
critical eye towards your own writing and question any word that
seems weak or out of place to see if you can find a stronger or more
appropriate one. It won't hurt a bit in the beginning if you make a list
of words that relate to what you are writing about. You might find a
thesaurus helpful until your imagination takes over. Here, in
summary, are the points covered in this chapter:

• Be discriminating in your choice of diction and use related words.
• Use specific rather than abstract language.
• Use strong verbs.

17

- Choose an unusual word occasionally for special effect.
- Keep a dictionary handy.

CONTEMPORARY LANGUAGE

The finest writers of any age are those whose writing reflects the times in which they live written in the language of their own day. This has been said before but it cannot be emphasized too strongly. You wouldn't dream of saying "Now fades the glimmering landscape on the sight." You'd say, "It's starting to get dark outside." Nor would you say

> If aught of oaten stop or pastoral song
> May hope, Chaste Eve, to soothe thy modest ear,

and so on. These lines from William Collins' "Ode to Evening," which is actually a very accomplished piece of poetry, sound quaint to us because of the outmoded language. We no longer use "thy" or "aught" nor do we refer to evening as a chaste maiden. Because English is as adaptable to change as any other convention, tired expressions are constantly being discarded in favor of freshness and innovation.

How responsive are you to change? Do you know what bill bissett is trying to do in his poetry or do you find you can't stand him? Do you write color without the *u* or do you still insist on the older spelling? The updating of language is a continuing process to which good writers are alert and to which the best of them contribute.

If you are a beginning writer, a good general rule for avoiding outdated language is to stick with phrases you and your friends use. Stay away from words you are not familiar with unless you want an unusual word for an unusual effect. If you imagine you are writing to a friend you will sound more natural. Casual conversational phrasing will enable you to resist unnatural contractions like *o'er* for *over* and *e'er* for *ever*. If you aren't in the habit of using such words in conversation, don't drag them into your writing. There is a nice conversational tone to this poem:

RETURN POSTAGE

This is going to be
a poem. You'll be able to tell because there'll be a lot
of page showing all around the words. You'll also be able to tell
because of the words; they will be highly ornamental, Rococo
even, like a Tiepolo ceiling. I don't write like
Creeley or Snyder — I like adjectives and
seriousness. I read Hallmark cards for inspiration. Every
afternoon, at lunchtime, I make phone calls to housewives all over
the city, gathering material for new poems. I'm wearing
a mask right now, I have to do that occasionally because

of my face. It never changes, not one line of it. It's like
an all-day sucker with the wrapping still on, something cherished
from childhood, from one special day when the circus was in
town and Daddy wasn't dead yet. Not artificial, mind you, but

lasting, the way my poems are, the way those cherubs in Tiepolo's
ceiling are.

Faye Kicknosway

Be on the lookout for contemporary expressions you can use in your writing. Better still, go out after them. If you need authentic dialogue — the conversation of persons younger than yourself or who move in a different milieu — go where such persons congregate. Hang around bars; ride in elevators; sit at lunch counters. And listen. There is a wonderful little vignette built around the conversation of college students in the pub scene in John Gardner's *October Light*. One can imagine the author sitting in a corner taking it all down while he was writing the book. Another writer who wanted the slang of high school students rode the city buses at four o'clock day after day. Sitting behind groups of students he got what he was after.

You can hear pithy little catch phrases around you all the time if your ears are tuned for them. Keep your notebook handy for jotting

20

these down along with your creative ideas. Common expressions like, "Funny thing about that girl," and "Oh, I would, I would in a minute," worked into poems by Leonard Cohen and Al Purdy respectively, keep their lines anchored to everyday language.

Current Slang

Al Purdy's "Oh I would [leave you], I would in a minute," has a ring to it that places it above "I love my wife but oh you kid," a slang expression that was popular a couple of generations ago. There is a distinction between informal language and slang, although both can be used to advantage. Slang is the result of an attempt to get more color into speaking and writing and it often adds great vitality to otherwise flat language. The problem with most slang is that it becomes dated too fast. Nobody now says, "twenty-three skiddoo." More recent expressions like "right on" and "groovy" have also become stale and will soon be discarded completely. You can use current slang if you are writing for immediate consumption only, and it does lend authenticity to certain kinds of dialogue, but standard English will last longer.

Dialect

Dialect, informal speech peculiar to one region rather than the country as a whole, presents special problems for the writer who wants to use it. Because Canada is made up of a variety of diverse peoples of different ethnic backgrounds, there is a wealth of rich speech differences here. But dialect, like slang, will root your writing in a certain time and place and may give rise to the charge of narrow regionalism, a target critics delight in sniping at. The following two poems bring two very different dialects, both Canadian.

An' when the circus cum around,
    He hitched his sleek old horses,
An' in his rattlin' waggon took
    His dimpled household forces —
The boys tew wonder at the clown
An' think his lot life's highest crown.

He wondered at the zebras wild,
    Nor knew 'em painted donkeys;
An' when he give the boys a dime
    Fur cakes to feed the monkeys,
He never thought in enny shape
He had descended frum an ape.

He never had an enemy
  But once a year, tew meetin',
When he and Deacon Maybee fought
  On questions of free seatin'
Or which should be the one t' rebuke
Pastor fur kissing' sister Luke.

Isabella Valency Crawford

You bad leetle boy, not moche you care
How busy you kipin' your poor gran'pere
Tryin' to stop you ev'ry day
Chasin' de hen aroun' de hay —
W'y don't you geev dem a chance to lay?
          Leetle Bateese!

Off on de fiel' you foller de plough
Den w'en you're tire you scare de cow
Sickin' de dog til dey jomp de wall
So de milk ain't good for not'ing at all
An' you only five an' a half dis fall,
          Leetle Bateese!

Too sleepy for sayin' de prayer tonight?
Never mind' I s'pose it'll be all right
Say dem tomorrow — ah dere he go!
Fas' asleep in a minute or so —
An' he'll stay lak' day til de rooster crow,
          Leetle Bateese!

But leetle Bateese! Please don't forget
We rader you're stayin' de small boy yet,
So chase de chicken and mak' dem scare
An' do w'at you lak' wit your ole gran'pere
For w'en you're beeg feller he won't be dere —
          Leetle Bateese!

One of the faults in both these excerpts is that the characters appear as stereotypes: Crawford's as the "country rube" and Drummond's as the "good" French-Canadian steeped in family, farm and church. Drummond's poem is saved from the patronizing attitude common to many dialect poems by this author's very real affection for the people he writes about. Literary tastes change from decade to decade, generation to generation. There is no longer the market for dialect poems there once was. This may be the reason Michel Tremblay debated a long time before deciding to use the *joual* of Quebec in his plays, yet when he did, they were well received and every one has since become a hit.

Dialect can be used to distinguish between the various voices in a play or story. It has been said that a writer needs to be a ventriloquist who can throw a different voice into each of his characters so they won't all sound as if one person — the author — is doing all the talking. Notice how differently these two characters from the same play, Shakespeare's *Henry IV, Part II*, speak. Each of them is addressing Sir John Falstaff.

Hostess: Tilly-fally, Sir John, ne'er tell me. Your ancient swaggerer comes not in my doors. I was before Master Tisick, the debuty, t'other day, and as he said to me, 'twas no longer ago than Wednesday last, "I' good faith, Neighbor Quickly," says he — Master Dumbe, our minister, was by then — "Neighbor Quickly," say he, "receive those that are civil, for" said he, "you are in an ill name." Now a' said so, I can tell whereupon. (II.iv.90-97)

King Henry: I know thee not, old man. Fall to thy prayers.
How ill white hairs become a fool and jester!
I have long dreamed of such a kind of man,
So surfeit-swelled, so old and so profane,
But being waked, I do despise my dream. (V.v.51-55)

Simplicity of Expression
Usually the less complicated the wording of your original thought, the more you will preserve its freshness and the better your writing will be. Among Canadian novelists, Morley Callaghan is the foremost example of the straightforward writer. His style — spare, unadulterated, unvarnished — is, like Ernest Hemingway's, partly the result of early training as a newspaper reporter. You can't get away with flowery writing on a newspaper. The great writers of every generation have had to drag language back down to earth when that of their contemporaries became too highflown and esoteric. Wordsworth wrote his manifesto setting out his aim to "speak a plainer and more emphatic language" for just that reason.

Today Tom Wayman, among others, is carrying on the tradition by getting away from the Establishment and writing poetry in contemporary language that the "guy on the street" can understand. The trend towards greater simplicity is evident in the work of any number of contemporary writers. If you compare Doris Lessing's awesome *Memoirs of a Survivor* to her earlier *Golden Notebook*, you will find the simpler writing style strikingly evident in the later work. An even more telling contrast can be seen in the work of E.L. Doctorow whose first novel, *The Book of Daniel*, contains long literary sentences and complex passages. But his second novel, *Ragtime*, exhibits a startling shift towards Hemingway's kind of simplicity. This is not to say that Doctorow sounds like Hemingway — far from it — but there is a noticeable lack of literary padding in both.

Craftsmanship, of course, does not mean simplicity to the exclusion of all else. There are any number of successful writers, Robertson Davies and Rudy Wiebe among them, whose works attest to the intricacy and diversity of the English language. But for the beginning writer, simplicity is a good concept to master before sailing into more complicated language waters. The trend is towards the shorter form whether in spelling, punctuation or contemporary language.

Trimming the Fat

It takes skill to know what to leave out as well as what to put in. Since fat language (verbosity) can hide the good bone structure in a piece of writing, pare the fat away. In other words, when you have said something once, stop. It isn't necessary to reinforce your ideas with flabby adjectives and adverbs. The following poem, good as it is, could be improved with a little judicious trimming.

> the world is late and summer
>   has arrived
>   without
>   the spring
> although
> I never said I love you out loud
>   I thought you knew
>   you ran

```
        too fast
    for my crippled words
            to follow
              I am
    left standing in muted silence
            as the
      juke box sings its solo
```

C.H. Molloy

There are some good things here, but does the poem really need the word "although?" What about "out loud?" And isn't "muted" saying the same thing as "silence?" When the verbal excesses are trimmed, the simply lovely expressions stand out more clearly. The supreme example of lines stripped to the bone in this century is Beckett's *Waiting for Godot*. You might not want to write as sparely as Beckett, but it takes skill to reach and maintain his kind of simplicity and make it work.

Summary
Taste in writing, like taste in furniture, is ultimately a matter of personal preference. As a beginning writer, even though you admire early Victorian more than streamlined functional, you will do better to stick with contemporary. After you have mastered the basics, you can go on to more elaborate writing. To sum up:

• Use contemporary language.
• Choose informal expression rather than slang unless you need slang for dialogue.
• Differentiate characters through speech differences.

TONE AND
WHAT IT SAYS

How do you tell someone that you no longer care and that it is all over between you? Do you say,

> *I hate you! Get out!*
> or
> *I no longer love you. Please leave.*
> or
> *Baby, I've had it with you. Get lost.*

Each set of words here displays a slightly different emotion from the others. Even though the intention of the speakers is the same, the range of feeling runs from fiery anger in the first to cool indifference in the third. Each tone is different. What we call tone takes its name from the emotional coloring of the speaker's voice and this in turn is determined by his attitude.

**TONE IS THE SPEAKER'S OR WRITER'S ATTITUDE
TOWARDS HIS SUBJECT, HIS AUDIENCE OR HIMSELF.**

In spoken language, the attitude of the speaker affects not only the tone of his expression but the meaning he conveys. Tone is therefore a very important clue to understanding what lies behind words, for words alone can be deceptive at times. If you ask a friend how he is and he answers "fine", you will rightly suspect differently if his voice is sad and his shoulders are slumped. His attitude says more than his words do. Similarly, if a teacher says to a class, "Well, aren't you a bright bunch," you know from his attitude and the tone of his voice he means the opposite.

Almost always in spoken language, the real attitude of the speaker can be detected in the inflections of his voice and these are backed up by his body language. In written language, the reader doesn't have these signs to guide him, he has only the words on the page. You, as the writer, have to reinforce your meaning with the tone of your writing. An appropriate tone is achieved mainly through the skilful use of diction.

Actually, everything in a piece of writing, including images, structure and rhythm, contributes to the tone, but diction has to be given first consideration. When all the words work well together they establish an emotional climate just as the signs in nature reveal the weather — dark clouds and a strong wind mean rain, and so on. In Emily Dickinson's poem, "After Great Pain a Formal Feeling Comes," the diction is perfectly consistent with the tone of numbed grief. A state of frozen emotion is a common one after the first shock following the news of, say, a death. If you have experienced such a shock yourself, you know that after the violent emotion subsides a numbness similar to physical freezing sets in. This after-emotion is captured in the poem through the diction,

> . . . This is the Hour of Lead —
> Remembered, if outlived,
> As freezing persons recollect the snow —
> First chill — then stupor — then the letting go —

Selecting the Tone
In the previous chapter, when we were discussing diction, we said that you, as a writer, can choose whatever words you please as long as they fit your meaning. As your skill develops, however, you will want words that are more than just suitable, you will want them to be consistent with the tone you are establishing. An experienced writer does even more than this. He decides on the tone *before* he starts to write. The novelist Joan Didion noted in an interview that if she gets the first line right, it sets the tone for the rest of the book. Most successful writers have such an overall view, and although the tone of a work can vary in places, there will be no major shift. So decide ahead of time on the tone you want to achieve and select or reject words for their effect on it.

In the short story "Snow" by Frederick Philip Grove, the depth of cold does not correspond, as in Emily Dickinson's poem, to the freezing of the human emotions following the news of a death. In Grove's story of a man frozen to death during a prairie blizzard, the title tells us that nature is the real protagonist. The tone, established in the first paragraph and sustained throughout, comes from a diction of realistic details describing the aftermath of a storm. It is not surprising that much of early Canadian fiction is concerned with weather when we consider the constant battle waged by the settlers against the harsh Canadian winters.

Major American writers, on the other hand, seem to have been more concerned with "inner" weather. Henry James captured the mental mood of his protagonist, the governess in "The Turn of the Screw," when she sees for the second time the figure of what she later learns is a ghost.

His face was close to the glass, yet the effect of this better view was, strangely, only to show me how intense the former had been. He remained but a few seconds — long enough to convince me he also saw and recognized; but it was as if I had been looking at him for years and had known him always. Something, however, happened this time that had not happened before; his stare into my face, through the glass and across the room, was as deep and hard as then, but it quitted me for a moment during which I could still watch it, see it fix successively several other things. On the spot there came to me the added shock of certitude that it was not for me he had come there. He had come for someone else.

The tone can shift in places throughout a long work but has to be consistent in a short one. In Tennyson's long poem *In Memorium*, written to commemorate the death of a close friend, the overall elegiac tone ranges from deep mourning, through acceptance, then doubt, and finally to hope of seeing his friend again after death. Death is a favorite subject with poets because it touches our deepest emotional roots, and a poem is, above everything else, an emotional expression. If we sometimes use poetry as self-therapy to get rid of inner misery in the face of tragedy, it can, as in Ariel's song in *The Tempest*, "suffer a sea-change into something rich and strange." For whatever reason, we continue to add to the preponderance of sad-toned poems in literature. Perhaps we don't write as often about happy moments because we want to live and prolong them, not get rid of them. At any rate, happiness is more difficult to write about than unhappiness. If you think this isn't so, try writing a completely happy poem.

28

For a culture madly devoted to the pursuit of pleasure, there is little evidence in contemporary literature that the chase is successful. Robert Frost, for example, wrote a great many poems with tragic undertones, but he wrote only one that mentions touching the blazing heights of joy. ("Happiness makes up in Height for what it Lacks in Length.") Although there aren't many completely happy poems, they do exist.

There are a number of emotions closely related to happiness — serenity, for example — that have found expression in verse form. Keats' "To Autumn" has generally been conceded one of the most flawlessly serene of all the great lyrics in English. Its tone comes from a blend of sense impressions. Beginning poets are usually satisfied to say, "ain't nature nice" with a visual picture only. Keats explored the effect of a warm autumn day on all the senses.

Diction (again)

Individual words are so important that if even one is out of character it can spoil the tone of an entire piece. In Theodore Roethke's poem "I Knew a Woman," if the poet had said "I knew a well-stacked woman" instead of "I knew a woman lovely in her bones," the adjective would have been completely out of place. As it is, the well-chosen "lovely" is the well-spring for the rest. Not only main words, but the seemingly unimportant *the's* and *ah's* and *oh's* can move the reader in ways that work below the level of conscious awareness. Note how, in the last stanza of Wordsworth's familiar Lucy poem, the word *oh* prepares us for what today we would call the punch line.

SHE DWELT AMONG THE UNTRODDEN WAYS

She dwelt among the untrodden ways
   Beside the springs of Dove,
A maid whom there were none to praise
   And very few to love;

A violet by a mossy stone
   Half-hidden from the eye!
Fair as a star when only one
   Is shining in the sky.

She lived unknown and few could know
When Lucy ceased to be;
But she is in her grave, and, oh,
The difference to me!

William Wordsworth

The little word *oh* has centuries of conditioning behind it, so closely
do we associate it with strong emotion. It has been used so often in
phrases like *Oh, no!* and *Oh, wow!* that it has become a cliché with an
exclamation mark. (How many love songs can you think of that
begin with *Oh?*) In Wordsworth's Lucy poem, it has a well-
calculated effect placed where it precedes the poignancy of the last
line. We are partially prepared, then swept into the emotional
ending where the whole poem is summed up in that word
"difference." Poignancy is a difficult tone to control if there is a
tendency on the writer's part to let the emotions run rampant. When
that happens you get bathos (sentimentality) instead of pathos.

Sentiment versus Sentimentality
Sentiment becomes sentimentality when the writer over-indulges in
emotion. The Victorians, who were given to excesses in a number of
strange ways, were very fond of tear-jerking lyrics, perhaps as a
release for emotions that had no healthier outlet. This is similar to
the phenomenon that takes place when you squeeze one end of a
blown-up balloon — the other end becomes distorted. And that is
just what happened to emotional expression in that peculiar age.
Whether the heroine was being tied to a railroad track, driven from
home in a snowstorm with her fatherless babe in her arms, or
married off to a rich old man, the audience loved having its feelings
manipulated on her behalf. Usually the pity being evoked was all out
of proportion to the situation. This is particularly evident in the
music-hall songs of the period.

A BIRD IN A GILDED CAGE

She's only a bird in a gilded cage
A beautiful sight to see
You may think she's happy and free from care
She's not, though she seems to be.

It's sad when you think of her wasted life
For youth cannot mate with age;
Her beauty was sold for an old man's gold,
She's a bird in a gilded cage.

Arthur J. Lamb

In the tawdry saloon where this song was tried out by Harry Von
Tilsen who wrote the music, several of the girls burst into tears — so
he knew he had a hit. Then, all over the country whenever a music-
hall singer emoted on stage and the piano vibrated with a tremulous
accompaniment, the audience would sob with pity for the poor little
rich girl. Today's sophisticated listener is more apt to chuckle than
weep at such sentimental indulgence. Emotion has to be genuine if it
is to outlast the idiosyncracies of fashion. One of the problems with
the poetry of the Nineties is that the pity elicited was really self-pity
— not concern for the other person. Sentimentality sidesteps the
complex issues of real human relationships. Although the girl in the
gilded cage lived in a palace, we are told her "wasted" life was "sad"
and that she was not "happy" — but nothing else in the poem
indicates this. The author *tells* us what to feel instead of letting the
poetry lead us towards this conclusion for ourselves. Blunt
statements about emotion are the mark of a lazy writer. *Never name
an emotion*. Let it come through instead in the tone of your work.

The observation that youth cannot mate with age — a debatable
issue, by the way — is also the theme of the miller's story in
Chaucer's *Canterbury Tales*. Chaucer gives us a picture of a high-
spirited girl married, like the girl in the gilded cage in the Victorian
song, to a man much older than herself. Here, in modern English, is
part of the opening section of "The Miller's Tale" describing Alison,
the young wife:

But of her song, it was as loud and lively
As any swallow sitting on a barn.
Furthermore, she could skip and play games
Like any calf or kid following its mother.
Her mouth was sweet as honey ale or mead
Or hoard of apples stored in hay or heather.
She was as skittish as a spirited colt.

Alison is a normal, lively, eighteen-year-old. Her husband is asking
for trouble when he tries to keep her, in Chaucer's words, in a

31

"narrow cage," especially with a handsome young university student living in the same house. And thereby hangs "The Miller's Tale." We are given such delightful sketches of the two young people that our sympathies fall naturally where the author wants them to.

Summary

Tone helps get your message across by puting the reader in a sympathetic mood. Every mood and every attribute of human nature has a tonal matchmate, and every one has been developed in literature at some time or other. There isn't an aspiring writer alive who knows Chaucer and Shakespeare who hasn't felt that these two masters between them "said it all" where human nature and human emotions are concerned. You really can't say much that is essentially different, but you can certainly say it your own way. And that is where tone will help you. These are the essential points to keep in mind:

• Strive for a controlling tone.
• If possible, decide ahead of time on the tone you want to achieve.
• Choose words that support this tone.
• Avoid telling the reader what to feel — let the tone suggest.

THEMES
AND THINGS

Creativity is an intense aliveness that brings into play nearly everything you are, including your psychic apparatus where ideas flow into other ideas. The original conception for a story or poem can come from any experience — the emotional upset of a quarrel, the preoccupation of reading the newspaper, or even shopping for groceries. What excites me into writing, however, may not move you at all. Reaction to experience is such an individual thing that no writer receives the same impressions as another or molds them quite the same way.

Sometimes, when an idea for a poem grips me and words pour out like water from a ruptured dam, I end up with pages and pages of tumbling undisciplined thoughts. At the first opportunity I sit down at the typewriter to turn them into a poem. When the writing is well under way I often find there is too much crammed into it. At this point I have to ask myself, "Just what are you writing about, anyway?" After separating the central idea from the others, I usually find in these cases I am writing not one poem but several. So I have to rescue the one I want to finish first.

Are you clear in your mind about what you want to say? If, like me, you are an untidy scribbler of thoughts at the start, pause before you get too far along and clarify your main idea. Write it out in one sentence or one word if you can. Then tape it to the wall above your typewriter where it will stare at you accusingly if you begin to surround it with a crowd of unrelated thoughts. But don't destroy those other ideas. You can use them somewhere else or turn them into different pieces later.

Once your main idea is firmed up, you can express it any way you want to. The unimaginative way is to make a bald statement of fact, but as Shelley said a long time ago, we have more facts now than we know what to do with. Art makes a fact or idea memorable. Most artists, including novelists and playwrights as well as poets, weave the important thought of a work in as its theme and this may be different than the surface meaning.

THE THEME OF A WORK IS ITS CENTRAL STATEMENT

In Shakespeare's *Measure for Measure*, the theme of capital punishment is presented in this moral problem: When a woman is offered the choice of saving a man's life (her brother's) at the price of her own virginity, what should she do? Supposing the brother has been killed (on the orders of the would-be seducer) should the state exact a life for a life? At the end of the play, the questions are partially resolved when justice is tempered with mercy. In this particular play, plot and theme are closely allied. But in *Hamlet*, in every way the most complex play ever written containing as it does so much of human experience, there are no cut-and-dried answers and no easy-to-express themes. The mystery of Hamlet's character remains the heart of the play. To borrow Hamlet's words, "The play's the thing" and the whole thing is the meaning.

Subject Matter

Is there anything you can't write about? Not today. No subject is taboo. You can say anything you want to, and if you say it well enough, some publisher somewhere will take a chance on you. (Let him worry about pornography or whatever.) As a beginning writer, though, you are probably more inclined to be reticent than overbold in expressing yourself, particularly where your innermost thoughts are concerned. Open the floodgates. If you can think it, you can say it. If you can say it, you can write about it.

How you write about it is our problem here. If you are uncomfortable with certain words or someone else's ideas, you still have a long way to go. But there is little point right at the start in forcing words or concepts which are unnatural for you. Your writing will come across as self-conscious and this in turn will make the reader uncomfortable. Use your emotional threshold as a criterion. If the excitement is running high, your words won't be self-conscious. Enthusiasm is the key. And the more you know about a subject, the more enthusiastic you will be.

Presenting your Subject

The ring of truth that comes from personal experience beats the best fiction going. Suppose you want to make a statement about war. If you were in Vietnam or Korea, fine, you can write about jungle warfare. If you weren't in the thick of the fighting write about your impressions of it *from where you were* at the time. Your own reaction to any experience will contain more genuine emotion than a made-up account no matter how many facts you can get hold of to put in it.

Many writers start with autobiographical material, sometimes disguised as fiction, sometimes not. To say that everyone has at least one novel in him isn't going far enough — there are countless ideas for books and poems in all of us depending on how the material is handled. Here's a tip for you: if you are writing autobiographically, don't write about what others have done to you — write about what you have done to them. There is more power in that once it has been released. You will end up with sentimentalism instead of real emotion if you try to sugar over unpleasant facts. Let them out. They make powerful themes. In his autobiographical poem, "The Circus Animals' Desertion," W.B. Yeats mentions some of the themes he developed over a long writing career — Irish mythology, the experiences of others, politics — but he says he found in the end he had to return to where the most powerful themes begin: the "foul rag and bone shop" of his own heart. This is where the pushed-out-of-sight experiences hide.

When anything is suppressed it festers and gathers explosive force. Which is why colonial states struggling for freedom from political overlords produce potent writers. The efforts of the Irish to gain independence from Britain at the beginning of this century gave rise to the literary renaissance to which Yeats contributed. For similar reasons, Quebec writers have produced what most critics feel is the best writing coming out of Canada today. Roch Carrier is one of the most talented of the younger Quebec writers. His brilliant little novel, *La Guerre, Yes Sir!*, concerns the arrival in a Quebec village of a young French-Canadian named Corriveau who was killed in the Second World War. The coffin is accompanied by English-Canadian soldiers, one of whom is killed by a villager. At the end of the story, the same flag that draped Corriveau's coffin is laid over the coffin of the dead Anglais. (A veiled appeal for Canadian unity?) Behind the plot, behind a universal statement about the great leveller death, is the explosive French-Canadian situation as it existed in Quebec during the war. No English-Canadian could have written this book.

35

I hope what has been said so far in this chapter about personal experience won't be construed as meaning you have to write about yourself. Writing *out of* experience is not necessarily the same as writing *about* it. Contemporary topics can be gleaned from newspaper clippings if you have the imagination to put yourself in another's place — to get inside his space — and the capacity to feel the situation with your own emotions.

Theme and Subject Matter
Theme and subject matter may be the same, but often they are not. The subject matter may be anything that points up and ullustrates the theme. In John Updike's novel, *Couples*, the subject matter can be expressed in one word: sex. But the theme is slightly different. The author defines it three-quarters of the way through the book as "the fate of us all, suspended in this one of those dark ages that visits mankind between millenia, between the death and rebirth of Gods, when there is nothing to steer by but sex and stoicism and the stars."

As in Updike's *Couples*, the subject matter in Brian Moore's *The Doctor's Wife* is sex. Moore's novel is built around a love affair between a married woman and a boy not many years older than her son. It is an absorbing account, with few plot complications, of a contemporary woman's struggle to free herself from an unsatisfactory marriage. The subject matter is sex; the theme is freedom. *Couples* and *The Doctor's Wife*: two novels with similar subject matter but different themes.

You certainly don't have to make a Socially Significant Statement if you are writing fiction or poetry, although many writers do. You don't have to make a statement of any kind. But at least let the reader in on what you are writing about. Keep your main idea clearly in front of you so that you too have something to steer by.

Titles
The old classroom advice about catching the reader's attention with the first line is even more applicable to the title. If you want the reader to open the cover of your book, you first have to interest him. Best sellers of recent years — *The French Lieutenant's Woman*, for example — bear this out. Critical praise helps too, of course. But Eric Segal's *Love Story* caught on in spite of its dismissal by the critics as a trite little tear-jerker. Its simple title touched a universal chord of sympathy in its audience. Usually, the simpler the title, the better.

A good title, if chosen early, can be the beacon that keeps you steering straight ahead. If your theme can be reduced to one or two words, that is your logical choice. Each of Arthur Hailey's titles — *Airport, Hotel, Wheels, The Moneychangers* — is a clear label of the book's contents. On the other hand, the title of Margaret Laurence's *Jest of God* was so amorphous it could have been about anything. Made into a film and renamed *Rachel, Rachel* it did well at the box office. A good title won't save a bad book or film, but it will lend added appeal to a good one.

Plot

Narrative poems, well-made plays, novels that tell a story — these have a beginning, a middle and an end. The writer plots his tale so that the incidents along the way add suspense and interest and in the last act or chapter the complications are resolved. A story-line is the most obvious means of moving a plot forward. The unfolding of events keeps the reader turning the pages to see what happens next. It can be as simple as boy-meets-girl, loses-girl, wins-girl-back. Or it can be as involved as an Arthur Hailey best-seller.

Arthur Hailey may not be the world's greatest novelist but he has been called the best plotmaker alive. A few years ago at a writer's conference I heard him explain his method of planning a novel. He tacks a large sheet of paper on the wall over his desk with the names of his characters and their involvements branching out across it. As the plot progresses and becomes more complicated he adds more sheets of paper until they stretch halfway around the room. He explained that this graphic method enables him to keep his characters separate and to see where they are going.

THINK OF YOUR PLOT AS A ROAD MAP TO A DESTINATION.
If you are a methodical writer you can plot your work from its conception so that, like Arthur Hailey, you are on track all the way. Or perhaps you prefer to let the ideas take you where they will for awhile. Whichever working method you use, your finished product should look as if you knew all along where you were going. The plot mapped out ahead will get you to the finish line safely.

All written material has plot even when nothing much happens in the narrative sense. Beckett's play, *Waiting for Godot*, doesn't tell a story. It doesn't even have a specific meaning as we usually think of that term. What it does is explore a situation, the human condition as seen by the playwright: we are always waiting for something to happen. Thus the play closes as it opened with the two tramps still waiting. The plot is circular.

In a descriptive poem or lyric where there is no story line, there is still a plot that moves the whole thing ahead. A poem has to get from line to line, stanza to stanza, beginning to end. In William Carlos Williams' "The Dance," the rhythmic movement of the poem leads "round and round" to a repetition of the opening line. The plot, as in *Waiting for Godot*, is circular. Repetition is a useful device for rounding off a plot.

The Writer's Vision

Stripped back to its naked seed, the urge to write grows out of the desire to share an experience. Experience itself can be a simple anyday happening or it can come from so many directions that it develops into a view of society at large. Writers who have something significant to say, from the Old Testament prophets to today's Mordecai Richlers, have all written out of such a view or vision. An encompassing vision gives great authority to a writer's themes.

Richler, who has twice won the Governor General's award for literature, calls himself a moral writer. He says he has been engaged with values and with honor almost from the beginning of his writing career. In a book like *St. Urbain's Horseman*, where the meanings are so diffuse they are almost impossible to extricate from the text, the theme defies simple definition, but the book is making a case for the middle-class, decent, bill-paying, honorable man. Even *Duddy Kravitz* and *Cocksure*, by implication, say something about honor. Disparate as the ingredients in Richler's novels may seem, they add up to an important statement about today's society.

The unexamined life is not worth living. Socrates' statement is as true today as when it was first made over two thousand years ago. Perhaps, if you haven't done so already, you might sit down some day soon and examine yourself and your life. Sort out your view and your philosophy of living. An overall view of your own life might lead to an overall view of life and society around you. Then you are on your way.

Summary

In this chapter we have covered some suggestions for different ways of representing an experience. Your communication can be as simple as a two-line poem or as complex as *St. Urbaine's Horseman* where the ideas flowing out of the experience defy simple presentation. When you come right down to it, the main enjoyment for the reader is not in the ideas or philosophy the work contains, but in the striking and original way the experience is presented. You want the reader to say, "Hey! That's how it is! I just never thought of it that way." Any deeper values in the work will be absorbed and retained along with the enjoyment.

- Write out of what you know (not necessarily *about* it.)
- Clarify your main idea and keep it in front of you while you are writing.
- Outline the plot before you get too far along.
- Aim at developing an overall philosophy for yourself.

IMAGERY

I remember attending a convocation one time at which the featured speaker advised the graduates not to put "water in the wine" as they set out on their careers — in other words, to stay true to their ideals. He started with the wine image and carried it through his speech, referring to it several times. I have forgotten most of the address, but I remember the image. An image stays in the reader's mind longer than a factual statement.

AN IMAGE IS A WORD-PICTURE USED BY A WRITER
TO ILLUSTRATE HIS THOUGHT.

Strictly speaking, an image can come from any sensory experience — hearing, touching, smelling, tasting — as well as from visual impressions. Actually there are something like 36 separate senses each with its own nerve pathway to the brain. You can capture any one of them in image. A train can be described as crying in the night, an old Ford as muttering its way down the road. Touch can be conveyed through the rough texture of tree bark, the cold shock of icy water, the soft surface of fine velvet. Try "polishing" silence, as Patrick Anderson does, as though silence were a "smooth white egg." Read Alice Munro's description of Leona Parry's dark overheated kitchen in the short story "The Time of Death" where you can smell the poverty. These are all sensory images, but for our purpose in discussing imagery and how to use it, the definition describing an image as a word-picture should serve.

Images, when they are used imaginatively, can enhance and

enliven whatever they illustrate. In Wordsworth's Lucy poem, the poet might have stopped short after saying Lucy was shy. That was the essential fact. But how dull. As we saw in the last chapter, poems and plays and stories are not written merely to communicate facts. The main interest for the reader lies in the memorable way the thought is presented. Whatever the subject matter, a good image will illuminate it.

Simile and Metaphor
When writers speak of images they usually mean simile or metaphor. A simile is a comparison that uses *like* or *as* to introduce the word-picture. When Wordsworth says Lucy was "fair *as* a star" he is using a simile. When he calls her a "violet by a mossy stone," he is using a metaphor. Both simile and metaphor compare things that are essentially unlike but have some characteristics in common. It doesn't take too great a stretch of imagination to see a city bus bearing down through traffic as a charging bull. Now, we all know that a bus isn't really a bull, but both are powerfully strong, both charge straight ahead, both make snorting sounds, and so on. By comparing the bus to a bull you can bring out the particular features of the bus that intensify the reader's mental picture of it. In the following examples, the last one is the most economical in that it incorporates the image into the verb.

- The bus charged through traffic like a bull.
- The bus was a bull charging through traffic.
- A bull of a bus charged through traffic.
- The bus bulled its way through traffic.

The last three are metaphors. A metaphor puts the image to work more directly than a simile does. For what it's worth, many writers today use similes sparingly and work directly from metaphors.

The fresher and more imaginative the image the more pleasure the reader will derive from the writing. Often you can spark up an old theme with new metaphors. Loneliness, for example, is one of the most overworked themes in modern literature. We could go into any number of reasons for modern man's loneliness and could analyze any number of plays, novels and poems written by authors who have responded to this familiar aspect of the human condition. On the surface it would seem difficult if not impossible to say anything fresh about loneliness at all. But W.H. Auden calls loneliness, in his poem of the same name, a "gate-crashing ghost," a "tactless gooseberry" and a "blackmailing brute." And a lot of other things besides. But he doesn't once mention the word *loneliness* in the poem. The pleasure in reading his poem is not in the meaning but in the metaphors.

Use of Detail

Adding concrete details is one way to sharpen an image. Snow, for example, can call up many different mental pictures unless it is pinned down by details that tell what sort is meant. Eskimos have twenty distinct and separate words for snow while we have only one. We can give it a precise texture by adding qualifying adjectives —wet snow, powdery snow, thick snow. Better still, we can describe it through an appropriate image. In his poem "Desert Places," Robert Frost works in descriptive details of snow falling on a field with only a few weeds and stubble showing through, with animals holed up in their lairs and the poet the only living thing in the darkening landscape. The detailed image gives a sombre picture of a snowcovered countryside and a much more chilling picture of loneliness than Auden's.

A passage that centres on sharp realistic detail can stamp almost as vivid a mental picture as a metaphor can. In his descriptions of places and characters, Dickens used a camera-eye technique of highlighting pertinent details. Remember his description of the schoolroom in Chapter One? The following is another of a series of connected images from the same novel desgined to show what the application of the utilitarian philosophy was doing to the environment of that day — which isn't so very different from what it is doing to our own.

[Coketown] was a town of machinery and tall chimneys out of which interminable serpents of smoke trailed themselves forever and ever, and never got uncoiled. It had a black canal in it, and a river than ran purple will ill-smelling dye, and vast piles of building full of windows where there was a rattling and a trembling all day long, and where the piston of the steam-engine worked monotonously up and down . . . .

This is straight reportorial writing. With the exception of the metaphor "serpents of smoke," it contains no poetic embellishment. Nevertheless, because of the vividness of the word-picture, it is as much an image as Auden's description of loneliness with its gate-crashing metaphors.

Imagery Sources

Dickens took his picture of Coketown from his immediate surroundings. Since England was going through the Industrial Revolution at that time, such scenes were common. On the other hand, Shakespeare drew much of his imagery from classical mythology because he was writing for an audience that for the most part was familiar with Greek gods and goddesses and all their retinue. Shakespeare could write of Prince Hal leaping onto his horse as if an angel dropped down from the clouds onto a fiery Pegasus because an educated Elizabethan would know immediately who Pegasus was. Chances are today's audience, if curious about the image, has to look up the mythological reference.

Use images your reader can relate to. The majority of today's population is urban dwelling and sees more of city or suburb streets than anything else. Doris Lessing's *Memoirs of a Survivor* derives much of its horror from the familiarity of the details which make her city of the near future frighteningly real. You will be creating a bond with your reader if, like Lessing, you stick with imagery that is familiar to most persons. You risk scaring your reader off or boring him if you lean too heavily on remote literary or mythological references. There is a wealth of real objects for images in any city scene, even if you are writing about unreality. If you describe imaginary gardens, at least put real toads in them, as Marianne Moore advised.

Clichés

A cliché is an expression that has been used so often it has become stale. It doesn't take much thought to rattle off clichés. They come to mind a little too easily. We have all said that something "leaks like a sieve" or is "dead as a doornail." These were original and expressive images at one time but they have been heard so often they have lost their effectiveness. Obvious clichés provoke the reader into impatience or boredom. Avoid them like — no, not like the plague — like boring politicians you aren't going to vote for. In place of worn out expressions practice substituting original images of your own. A little thought can transform "leaks like a sieve" into "leaks like a rusty eavestrough," "dead as a doornail" into "dead as an old Dodge without a battery."

A successful image will cause the reader to feel a thrill of surprise and pleasure. The main objection to clichés is that they have lost the power to do this. They are the product of an unimaginative mind. It takes a sharpened awareness and a little practice to devise original images like those Auden uses. You won't find one lazy or sloppy cliché in his poem.

Relevance of Images

Images and the detail in them should relate to the idea you want to express. If they wander off aimlessly in any direction, or point the reader the wrong way, your focus will be blurred and your meaning may be lost. Just as you need suitable words to express your ideas, you also need suitable images. Discard any that are weak or inappropriate and put your imagination to work to devise better ones.

Images are inappropriate when they contradict the meaning they are meant to illustrate or when they bring out the wrong qualities. Suppose you want to portray something ugly, say a noisy snowmobile ruining a beautiful snowy landscape. You might be tempted to write, "It purrs across the landscape like a well-fed cat." Now, the image of a cat isn't a bad one, and certainly the sound of a well-oiled machine can be likened to the purring of a contented cat. But "purring" and "well-fed" are not qualities relevant to ugliness. A snarling animal with its claws out is apt to do more damage than a contented one. Let's change the image to,

It snarls across the landscape like a sharp-clawed cat.

In Henry James' short story, "The Beast in the Jungle," there is an image that illustrates the relevance of images. The title of this story is ironic in that the beast, the tiger of experience, never does spring for John Marcher and never burns bright like the tiger in Blake's poem. In the scene where the woman who has loved Marcher unrequitedly for years comes very close to declaring her passion, he does not respond. He is shown standing by the fireplace which is "fireless and sparely adorned." Marcher is also fireless, without warmth or ardor. If there had been live flames leaping in the fireplace, the image and the theme would have pulled against each other. As it is, the cold fireplace is appropriate.

Another image that carries the theme within it can be found in Margaret Laurence's "The Loons," one of the short stories that form the novel *Bird in the House*. At the end of "The Loons," Vanessa, who is telling the story, is sitting on the new government dock which juts out into the lake where her parents used to have their summer cottage and where she played as a child with a crippled Indian girl, Picquette Tonnere. She describes the changes that have affected the lake through the encroachment of a shoddy culture of neon signs and resort hotels. At night the lake, darkly shining, seems the same but everything is quiet — too quiet. The loons are no longer there. The image of the loons at the beginning of the story and their death-like absence at the end is paralleled by the death of Picquette. The loons provide a haunting and provocative mirror image of the theme.

In the work of a great writer the imagery pattern is always related in some way to the theme. In *Hamlet*, the imagery is of disease and corruption because "something is rotten in the State of Denmark." And in *Anthony and Cleopatra* where worlds are being fought for, the dominating image is of magnificence and vastness. Antony is the "demi-Atlas of this earth" and the "triple pillar of the world." Caroline Spurgeon makes these observations in her classic study, *Shakespeare's Imagery and What it tells us*. Imagery that is closely related to the theme adds depth to the meaning.

Defining character through Imagery
Relevant images are a sure-fire way of adding color to any character you are developing. Look how Shakespeare gives the audience an instant introduction to Falstaff, the great ebullient lover of the pleasures of the flesh. This is the opening dialogue in the scene where we first meet the fat knight:

> *Falstaff:* Now, Hal, what time of day is it, lad?
> *Prince Hal:* Thou art so fat-witted, with drinking of old sack, and unbuttoning thee after supper, and sleeping upon benches after noon, that thou has forgotten to demand that truly which thou wouldst truly know. What a devil hast thou to do with the time of day? Unless hours were cups of sack, and minutes capons, and clocks the tongues of bawds, and dials the signs of leaping houses, and the blessed sun himself a fair hot wench in flame-coloured taffeta — I see no reason why thou shouldst be so superfluous as to demand the time of day.

Who but a poet would think of calling minutes "capons" and the sun a "fair hot wench" in a red dress? These are more that startling images; each defines Falstaff by relating to his lusts. Similarly in Joseph Heller's *Catch-22*, the classic anti-war novel of this century, the men are characterized by the accompanying imagery. Hungry Joe is described, for example, as having a desolate face "like an abandoned mining town."

Film Images

Films, because they are a visual medium, are a natural for artistic images. One of the most famous of all film images occurs at the end of *All Quiet on the Western Front* when Paul, the young German soldier, is shot as he reaches for a butterfly. We see the butterfly land; we see the sniper take aim. All we see of Paul is his hand stretching out. The sniper fires; the hand twitches, then drops. In this fine film and others like it, such images set them apart from the usual run-of-the-mill hollywood offerings.

In a more recent film, *The Late Show*, Art Carney and Lily Tomlin are involved in a series of murders and other horrors in the city of Hollywood. As the film closes we see them sitting on a bench waiting for a bus. The back of the bench carries a Wax Museum advertisement featuring the face of the familiar Frankenstein monster. In the emotionally understated dialogue, the relationship that has been developing between the two principals is finally pledged. Then the bus pulls in blocking our vision. When it leaves, the bench is empty. The protagonists have gone on to a new life together leaving the horrors of the past in the past just as the Frankenstein monster has been relegated to wax museums and old late-night shows. But the bus, the tentative lovers and their relationship are all alive and moving. All this is implied in the closing image.

Thinking in Images

One of the keys to becoming a more imaginative writer is to start thinking in images. Children are especially good at this because their imagination has not yet been stifled by the everyday world. Remember how, as a child, you saw castles in clouds, bears in dark bushes and giants everywhere? Poets have retained this gift. Joni Mitchell carries cloud images into "Both Sides Now." Starting with simple child-like images of "ice-cream castles in the air," the lyric ends with clouds that only "rain and snow on everyone." Clouds become a metaphor for life encompassing both the magic and the disillusion.

Thinking in images might not be easy at first. If they don't flow naturally you can unblock your imagination by making comparisons between familiar objects and less ordinary ones. (Seeing a bus as a bull.) You can speed the process by analyzing images in films and in the work of other writers. It takes practice to become a skilled image-maker, but once you start looking for them, images will suggest themselves.

Summary

Images are a distinctive and essential element of all art forms. This is especially true of poetry but applies to other forms of writing as well. In fiction, they are a major clue to meaning, character and mood. Images will do more than any other single factor to make your writing memorable and should therefore be looked on as one of the most valuable tools in your creative-writer's workbox.

- Use images to make your writing more vivid.
- Use images the reader can relate to.
- Avoid Clichés.
- Tie your images to each other and to your meanings.

SYMBOLISM

In the previous chapter we saw how images can add meaning to a poem or a prose paragraph by comparing one thing to another. The violet in Wordsworth's Lucy poem indicates that Lucy was a shy person because the idea of shyness nearly always comes to mind when this flower is mentioned, so much so that shrinking violet is a common synonym for a self-effacing person. (We know Wordsworth doesn't mean Lucy was purple-petalled.) Similarly, when a writer says someone has heart, we know he is referring to compassion and not to the blood-pumping organ in the chest. When the church is mentioned, it usually stands for organized religion rather than one particular building with four walls a roof and a steeple. Any image that becomes firmly associated with a certain concept becomes a symbol for that concept.

> A SYMBOL IS AN OBJECT THAT STANDS FOR SOMETHING ELSE
> AND THAT HAS ACQUIRED MORE MEANING THAN THE LITERAL
> DEFINITION OF THE OBJECT INDICATES.

A person as well as an object can serve as a symbol. In E.L. Doctorow's best-selling novel *Ragtime*, several of the leading characters have no names. They are identified only as Mother, Father, Mother's Younger Brother, and so on. The social changes these characters experience over the early decades of this centry are those that have affected every American family since. This, along with the lack of individual names, gives Doctorow's family members wider-ranging importance than is generally attached to fictional characters. They are focal points for the historic events depicted in the novel and can be seen as symbols of the American family.

Actually, all words as such, whether written or spoken, are symbols. *Tree* stands for an object with trunk, branches and leaves only because we transform the word into the visual counterpart in our minds. Such a symbol means nothing to someone who speaks no English. On the other hand, good literary images and symbols carry their meaning with them even when translated into another language. In literature, writer and reader can speak the same language with symbols that have a commonly accepted meaning.

Universal Symbols

As a rule, the more familiar the symbol the more accessible the writer's meaning. In Pablo Neruda's "Sonata: There's No Forgetting," the "black night" he speaks of has a long metaphorical history stretching back to the "black night of the soul," an expression that originated with St. John of the Cross, a Spanish mystic and poet of the Sixteenth Century. John's dark night stood for the trials of the soul in its journey through life. The image, which has become a universal symbol for suffering and despair, has now passed into other languages. Neruda's poem is full of familiar symbols, almost all of which are fully comprehensible translated into any language.

SONATA: THERE'S NO FORGETTING

If you should ask me where I've been
I must reply: "It happens."
I must speak of the soil obscured by the stones,
Of the river destroyed while still existing.
I know only things that birds lose,
The ocean left behind, or my weeping sister.
Why are there so many regions? Why does one day
Join with another day? Why does a black night
Accumulate in the mouth? Why do the dead exist?

All that have passed have not been memories,
Nor is what sleeps in forgetfulness a yellow dove,
But rather, faces wet with tears,
Fingers at the throat,
And all that collapses from the leaves;
The obscurity of a day gone by,
A day fed with our sad blood.

I'll show you violets, swallows,
And all that pleases us and appears
On the pretty large postcards
Sent back from places that time and sweetness visit on
their trip.
But let's not penetrate beyond the teeth.
Let's not chew on the husks that silence accumulates.
Because I don't know what to answer:
There are so many dead,
And so many seagulls that the red sun has damaged,
And so many heads that the ships strike,
And so many hands that have imprisoned kisses,
And so many things that I want to forget.

Pablo Neruda

In his poem, Neruda refers to his country as covered with stones and he speaks of a river as having been destroyed. Earth and river are traditional symbols for life, whereas stones are hard, cold, heavy and as death-dealing as the hand of a tyrant. There are birds in the poem. Birds commonly symbolize freedom (free as a bird) which is lost under a dictatorship. If you know anything of Neruda's political background you will have little trouble interpreting his symbols. His poem has far more emotional power than a political diatribe, no matter how impassioned, and will almost certainly be remembered longer.

For similar reasons, the use of commonly understood symbols when incorporated into the action on stage moves us in ways impossible to achieve by recitation of lines alone. Great actresses and actors know this and accompany their words with symbolic gestures. At the end of *Measure for Measure*, when it was produced at Stratford, Ontario, in 1975, Martha Henry as the sanctimonious Isabella paused at the very end of the play and all alone on the stage took off the glasses she had been wearing throughout the performance. Then, turning slowly and thoughtfully, she gazed around with a new look of wonder on her face. She was seeing things differently.

Many novelists weave symbolism into the theme as part of its basic fabric. In John Updike's *Couples*, the church which burns down at the end is the traditional symbol for religion. Here and there in the novel there have been references to the passing of Christianity in such images as the faces of the occupants of a car looking like dead saints under glass. In the fictional town of Tarbox, extramarital sex has become the foremost preoccupation of the adults, eventually corrupting everyone in the place including the almost saintly Angela. Through its symbols the novel is saying that sex has become the new religion and is now the centre of the town's social activities, a role once filled by the church. The destruction of the church at the end is therefore highly symbolic.

Animal Symbolism

Animals and insects have had symbolic natures tacked onto them from ancient times. *Aesop's Fables* are 2500 years old yet the human attributes of his animals have stuck to this day. The fox still exemplifies cunning ("The Fox and the Grapes"). Through the ages we have continued to endow the lion with kingliness, the rat with deceit, the wolf with viciousness. The wolf in "Little Red Ridinghood" is the typical symbol. Modern writers like Farley Mowat have tried with limited success to change the image of some of the more maligned creatures, but a symbol is difficult to defeat. The snake, even the beneficial garden snake, remains a symbol for repulsiveness. Fear of snakes has been so bred into our bones that most people shudder at sight of them. And like Little Miss Muffet who was frightened when a spider sat down beside her, we also recoil from spiders. We have attached a symbolic nature to them, too.

Nature Symbolism

As pointed out in the comment on Neruda's poem, the nature-symbols of earth, river and stones are common to all languages and literatures. An event like the political takeover of a country is topical and subject to change but nature is eternal. Symbols rooted in nature have lasting significance. Water in any form — ocean, sea, river, rain — is traditionally the life-giving element. The sea stands for eternity, the river for flux. Spring symbolizes life and rebirth, winter means death. These symbols go back to the dawn of civilization and the earliest religions which were nature-oriented.

A notable instance of nature-symbolism occurs in Shakespeare's history plays where the image of the untended garden, used over and over and tied to England's early kings, comes to symbolize political mismanagement and corruption. The symbol reaches its peak in *Richard II*.

> . . . our sea-walled garden, the whole land,
> Is full of weeds; her fairest flowers chok'd up,
> Her fruit trees all unprun'd, her hedges ruined,
> Her knots disorder'd, and her wholesome herbs
> Swarming with caterpillars. (III.iv.43-47)

The image of the neglected garden, appearing in different settings and picking up additional meaning each time, stands for the whole country, something of far greater importance than one garden alone. We don't need a political scandal of Watergate proportions to show us how appropriate Shakespeare's symbol still is. When the head gardener is corrupt, the whole garden suffers. Such corruption invariably creeps down through all levels of government until the entire country is full of weeds and swarming with caterpillars.

Flower Symbolism
There is a very old but familiar proverb that says if a starving man finds two pennies let him spend one for bread and one for a rose. We aren't meant to take such advice literally; "bread" and "rose" are symbols — the one, food for the body; the other, food for the soul. In nearly every language, flowers, particularly roses, symbolize beauty. Long before Edmund Waller's poem appeared in the Seventeenth Century, roses were sent to beautiful women as emissaries of love, and they still perform this pleasant task as any florist can testify.

SONG

> Go, lovely rose,
> Tell her that wastes her time and me,
> That now she knows,
> When I resemble her to thee,
> How sweet and fair she seems to be.

> Tell her that's young,
> And shuns to have her graces spied,
> That hadst thou sprung
> In deserts where no men abide,
> Thou must have uncommended died.

Small is the worth
Of beauty from the light retir'd:
　　Bid her come forth,
Suffer herself to be desir'd
And not blush so to be admired.

　　Then die, that she
The common fate of all things rare
　　May read in thee,
How small a part of time they share,
That are so wondrous sweet and fair.

The coupling of hearts and flowers has been overworked to the point
of sentimental cliché. Thus it is easy to burlesque. A love scene
played to the accompaniment of the Victorian tune "Hearts and
Flowers" is sure to raise hoots of laughter. It is risky for today's
writer to use roses to symbolize love or beauty *except as a jumping-
off point* for a more imaginative treatment. Even roses with thorns
and worms in the bud have been done to death. If you are going to use
flowers as representative of anything, you had better come up with
some that haven't been wilted through overhandling.

Color Symbolism
Colors can be fascinating and complex symbols. Color psychologists
tell us our reactions to color are partly innate, partly learned. Normal
babies, when presented with a choice of toys of different colors, will
choose red because it is the most stimulating of all the colors in the
spectrum. Ask four or five friends to free-associate (name the first
thing that comes to mind) when you say *red* and you will get answers
that indicate passion, danger, anger or fire. Some people are in their
element with red. Others, for personal reasons, can't stand it. If you
were repeatedly tormented by a bully in a red sweater when you were
a child, you probably hate red. This is a conditioned or personal
response.

　　Traditional color associations, on the other hand, have a long
history of symbolism going back to the Middle Ages and beyond. In
Chaucer's day there was an accepted code of color meanings that
enabled the readers of *The Canterbury Tales* to deduce the character
traits of the pilgrims with no trouble at all. Their physical coloring
and the color of the clothes they wore gave them away. The lusty
nature of the Wife of Bath is symbolized by her fine scarlet stockings
and her face which was fair and red of hue. These hints support the

fact that she has had five husbands already and is on the pilgrimmage to look for husband number six.

Although the symbolism of individual colors has been weakened in our day by being spread over a more complex range of meanings, some colors still have widely accepted connotations. We tend to associate white with purity, green with growth and yellow with sunshine. Black usually indicates deep depression, but to a black person black has a whole new dignity and beauty. Color meanings change from culture to culture and decade to decade. In the old westerns the villain always wore a black hat, the hero a white one. Today no such color certainty exists and the villain may just as readily be dressed in white as in any other color. If you intend colors to carry symbolic overtones in your writing you will have to give the reader additional clues. The following poem makes good use of traditional white and green but the symbolism is backed up by other details.

THIS ROOM

The white flowers unpetal, their stems
wither from an absence of leaves

This room barrens them,
its single window, coloured glass
whose light she worships
as if it were more than art,
more than a relief

The flowers are not content with that

They crave colours that are real,
seek a sunlight touched only by air

The water she pours on them
can never be rain
and the dust-ridden floor
has never known green;
on the wall the butterflies
are angled downward, will not fly again

The white flowers are dead

Oblivious
she sits crosslegged in a corner,
draws wings on her wrists with a feather pen,
doesn't notice the sun's descent
pressing her face
into a pattern of coloured glass

Eva Tihanyi

Freudian Symbols

Freudian symbolism, in which all long tapered objects are phallic symbols and all dark openings and enclosures their feminine counterparts, enjoyed a literary vogue a few decades back. Now that Freud's stock has been falling on the psychology market, overt Freudian symbols in literature appear dated. If you plan to use textbook terms of any kind in literature, one of the problems you face — beyond the narrowness of the terminology — is their early aging. Like any literary device, symbolism can be carried to extremes. When someone asked Freud if his cigar was a Freudian symbol, he replied sharply that sometimes a cigar is just a cigar.

Personal Symbols

Writers sometimes begin with a traditional symbol and move it into a more personal range of meaning. Private symbols, when used successfully, work through fresh suggestion rather than leaning on accepted associations. In Blake's poem, the rose — the usual stand-in for love and beauty — has been turned into something ugly.

THE SICK ROSE

O rose, thou art sick!
The invisible worm
That flies in the night,
In the howling storm,

Has found out thy bed
Of crimson joy
And his dark secret love
Does thy life destroy.

We are led by the sexual images in the poem, "bed" "joy" and "love", to see Blake's rose as a personal symbol for physical love which ought to be a joyous experience but which is being blighted by a poison of some kind. We aren't told what the poison — the "dark secret" is. It might be prudery, deceit, jealousy, suspicion or whatever the reader's own experience or imagination bring to it. To some students of Blake, the "worm", which is an ancient symbol for snake and so for Satan, brings sin and the Church into the act. Thus the poison is tied to the teachings of the Church of the time: that sex except for purposes of procreation was sinful. But any number of other interpretations are possible. One of the attributes of private symbols like Blake's is that they cannot be held to a single and specific meaning. They suggest possibilities instead of stating positives.

Any object can pick up symbolic overtones through repeated appearances in a writer's work. Empty chairs, brought on stage in increasing numbers in Ionescu's *The Chairs*, express a number of things: the horror of proliferation, failure to communicate and the inability to transmit experience to posterity. These themes are intertwined with others throughout the plot in which an old man and woman have invited a group of distinguished visitors to hear the message the old man wants to leave. The couple keep up a stream of conversation with the guests — who are never seen or heard — as more and more empty chairs are placed on stage. The chairs are a poetic symbol for emptiness and futility, the author's philosophy of Absurdism. Because Ionescu's vision transforms an ordinary object into a extraordinary symbol, we are forced to acknowledge his philosophy: in the end everything is futile. (We don't necessarily have to adopt it as our own.)

Summary
Symbolism is a difficult tool to use at all, let alone use well. Do you really need it in your writer's toolbox? You can build a plain sturdy piece of furniture if that is what your taste prefers, or you can decorate the whole piece as intricately as a hand-carved Haitian chest. All kinds of art have their buyers. But in writing, when a symbol works well, when it challenges the reader and leaves him as an image does with the staying power of a visual object, then it is an invaluable literary device for making the writer's thought more memorable. Almost everything said in the previous chapter about images applies also to symbols. The two additional points made in this chapter are:

• Universal symbols have readily accepted meanings.
• Private symbols need further clues for the reader.

MYTH

It's like this: It's the first nice day of spring after a long hard winter; with the sun warm on your back and the breeze soft on your cheek, you feel a lifting of spirits and a resurgence of energy. You decide to walk to work this morning instead of driving. As you swing down the sidewalk you notice the first green is showing through the dead brown spears of grass on the neighborhood lawns and here and there the spring bulbs are beginning to push up from their winter dormancy. Nature is coming to life again after her long sojourn in the land of the dead.

What you have been witnessing, indeed what your spirits are part of at this time of year, is a re-enactment of the Demeter myth. In the story, Demeter, Greek goddess of the cornfields, had a beautiful daughter named Persephone. One day while Persephone was picking flowers in a meadow, the god of the underworld abducted her and took her down to the nether regions. Demeter was so angry she decreed that nothing should grow until she got her daughter back. All vegetation disappeared from the earth. Zeus, the father of the gods, was worried that the race of men would die too unless Demeter repented. So he went to the king of the underworld, his brother, to negotiate the girl's return. The upshot was that Persephone, who had eaten some of the food of the dead, had to spend some months each year with the god of the underworld but could return to her mother for the other months. Each time she comes back we have spring.

The Demeter myth was an ancient Greek version of the turn of the seasons. The story is found in different forms in a number of lands where the difference between summer and winter is sufficiently pronounced to illustrate the theme of death and resurrection. The awakening of spring corresponds not only to Persephone's return from the underworld, but also, in the German legend, to the rescue of Brynhild who sleeps within flaming walls until Siegried comes. There is also a Hindu myth about a girl who lies in a palace of glass behind seven walls of spears. And we are all familiar with the fairy tale of the sleeping beauty. In each of these accounts the heroine lies in a sleep like death until she is rescued by a hero who symbolizes the sun returning with strength and life to break the chains of winter and free her. You will probably also recognize some features of the myth in the Christian account of the resurrection which is celebrated, significantly, near the spring equinox.

The most important element in any myth is *the truth that is embedded in it*. The spring miracle of rebirth continues to testify to the truth behind the Demeter story. Myth is sometimes used in a rather loose sense to mean a fallacy as when we speak of the myth of American superiority or the myth of women's limitations, but this usage, although sanctioned by some dictionaries, is an injustice to the original definition. The great myths were always woven into a story that was attempting to explain a phenomenon that was otherwise unexplainable at the time.

A MYTH IS A CULTURAL TRUTH EMBODIED IN A NARRATIVE THAT
TRIES TO EXPLAIN WHY THE WORLD IS AS IT IS AND WHY THINGS
HAPPEN AS THEY DO.

The need to mythologize seems to be inherent in all races. C.G. Jung, one of the great pioneering psychologists of the first half of this century, tried to explain this need by theorizing that man has a collective subconscious, as well as an individual one, in which common racial symbols have been deposited. He believed that these symbols were predispositions in primitive man for experiencing and responding to his world and were passed on to succeeding generations much as basic body features are. He called the symbols, some forty of which he identified, archetypes of the collective unconscious. Whether or not you hold with Jung regarding the archetypes, there are quite a number of common symbols that appear in the myths of different peoples around the world.

The old myths have untold centuries of acceptance behind them. Unlike a personal symbol, a true myth cannot be fashioned by any one writer; it grows out of the culture of the race. Or, if you ascribe to Jung's theory, out of the collective subconscious. A few recent writers, notably William Faulkner whose novels of Yoknapatapha County portray in narrative form the impact of American Industrial Society on the old South, have captured the essence of modern myth in their work. If you believe, as many do, that American Industrial Progress is the Great God of Western civilization, then Faulkner did indeed hit on one of the significant myths of our time. The Canadian novelist Dave Godfrey carried this myth even further in *The New Ancestors* by exploring the impact of American industrial progress on the peoples of Africa.

Greek Myth
A reader who is familiar with Greek myths can find them in any number of modern writings. The foremost example is probably James Joyce's *Ulysses* in which incidents of one day in turn-of-the-century Dublin parallel events in the original Odyssey. The wanderings of the Greek hero make a marvellous structure for Joyce's story. Ulysses is one version of a common myth involving a hero on a quest of some kind. The hero has appeared as Perseus, Prometheus, David, Jack the Giantkiller, St. George and even as the space heroes of Apollo 11 landing on the moon, an observation made by Time Magazine. The Hero's name is legion, his quest never-ending. Tennyson incorporated man's insatiable thirst for adventure — the basic truth behind the myth of the hero — in these line from his poem "Ulysses":

> I cannot rest from travel: I will drink
> Life to the lees. All times I have enjoy'd
> Greatly, have suffer'd greatly, both with those
> That loved me, and alone; on shore, and when
> Thro scudding drifts the rainy Hyades
> Vex the dim seas. I am become a name
> For always roaming with a hungry heart.

Although the questing hero is one of the most prominent figures of Greek myth to appear in modern literature, there are others that can be found in various settings. John Updike incorporated one of the old Greek figures into *The Centaur* which mixes myth and reality so thoroughly they become one.

The myths and stories of the old Testament underly a great deal of English literature just as the Greek myths do. In spite of the fact that we are no longer as familiar with the Bible stories as earlier generations were, the Bible remains one of the world's best sellers. There is still a sizeable audience for Biblical allusions. The elements of universal myth can be found in the story of Adam and Eve.

> And the Lord God planted a garden eastward in Eden; and there he put the man whom he had formed . . . and his wife Eve. And God said, Of every tree of the garden thou mayest freely eat, but of the tree of knowledge thou shalt not eat. Now the serpent was more subtle than any beast of the field and he said unto the woman, in the day ye eat thereof, then your eyes shall be opened and ye shall be as gods. . . , and she took of the fruit thereof and did eat, and gave also unto her husband with her; and he did eat. And the eyes of them both were opened. . . . Therefore God sent them forth from the garden of Eden and placed a flaming sword to keep the way. (*from the St. James version of The Bible*)

Taken at surface value, the story of the Garden of Eden is the Jewish and Christian version of the creation of the world. The religious belief was built into a narrative for a people who lived before the theory of evolution was evolved. Most cultures have a similar creation myth.

On another level, however, the story of Adam and Eve is a maturation myth illustrating a common fact of life: we grow up, or in literary terms, progress from innocence to experience. As a symbolic representation of how we go from one stage of life to another, the Garden of Eden represents childhood or the time of innocence, and life after eating of the tree of knowledge symbolizes adulthood or the state of experience. Much of adult knowledge, even if not actually forbidden when we are children, is incomprehensible at that time of life. Our religious forefathers, considering a little knowledge a dangerous thing, attached the sins of pride and disobedience to the myth. As we become more knowledgeable we are better able to handle life's experiences. We cannot, of course, go back to a state of childlike innocence again.

The innocence-to-experience theme is a very common one in literature. It underlies Constance Beresford-Howe's novel, *The Book of Eve* whose heroine leaves the sheltered life of her husband's house

— a very restricted Eden — and strikes out on her own with her first old age pension cheque. It's a delightful tale of the experiences of an eccentric and unusual Eve. The Garden of Eden, Eve, the Fall from grace — these have been used perhaps more often in literature than other biblical myths. But most of the Old Testament Prophets have come in for a share of mythologized prominence and so have the Jezebels and Delilahs. There is a rich mine of symbols in the Bible.

Folk Tales and Fairy Tales

Jung found many of his mythic archetypes in various forms in the old European folk and fairy tales. One of the commonest symbols is the mother archetype. She may be associated with goodness and fertility or she may symbolize destructive forces. As an evil symbol she appears as the witch in Hansel and Gretel and as the evil stepmother in Snow White and the Seven Dwarfs.

The hero, whom we discussed a few paragraphs back, is another universal figure who appears frequently in fairy tales. He may appear as the Prince who wakens a Sleeping Beauty, rescues an imprisoned princess or marries a Cinderella. Or he may be a mysterious person with the power to rid a town of rats and steal its children. He may appear as Everyman, a little guy not unlike ourselves, whose heroic aspirations lead him to find fame and fortune by overcoming giant-sized odds. Fairy tales, like myths, retain their relevance because of the universal truths embodied in them.

Canadian Myth

Since we are part of Western Civilization we share its inherited cultural myths. Do we have a distinctive Canadian myth? Only time will tell. At present there are two elements in our national background that seem destined for mythic significance: the unique character of the Canadian landscape and the French-English split. The first of these is what Northrop Frye called the mythopoeic strain growing out of the experience of settling a land so vast that he wonders if any other national consciousness has had "so large an amount of the unknown, the unrealized, the humanly undigested," built into it. Hugh MacLennan and Roch Carrier have each attempted to mythologize in their work the French-English split.

Not much has been done in this country towards incorporating into Canadian literature the myths of the Native Peoples. Although many of the Indian and Eskimo myths have been collected — mostly by white writers — in book form, they have not yet appeared to any extent in the literature of the country. Since myth has to be felt in the very marrow of one's bones, what is needed is a native writer steeped in his own culture and talented enough to preserve the myths in literature the way Norval Morriseau has immortalized them in his paintings.

History and legend are further sources for myth. Riel, the legendary Métis — patriot or traitor, depending on which side of the fence you view him from — has all the qualities of a mythic hero as he continues to trouble our national split personality. Canadian history has many mythic figures like Riel whose stature we are only just beginning to appreciate. James Reaney found the stuff of myth in the legends surrounding the Donnellys of Lucan, Ontario. He turned their story into a series of stage plays with the flavor of Greek tragedy. And Margaret Atwood has invested Susanna Moodie with myth in *The Journals of Susanna Moodie*, maintaining through Mrs. Moodie's voice that the wilderness experience is still alive in us.

Summary

We are not, on the whole, a myth-conscious people. We look at the world more and more through the eyes of science and industry, but then these in themselves, as more than one writer has demonstrated, have become the Great Gods of our culture. Our writers have also demonstrated that such gods are unsatisfactory because both the spiritual and the rooted aspect is missing. As Jung pointed out, man is still part of nature, is still connected to his own roots, and a society that cuts him off from his roots is not only no culture but a prison. Perhaps what we need for this age is a new mythology to which the majority of persons, particularly the writers, can subscribe. Until then, the old myths are still there, still operable, as background material.

• Myths are important for the truths behind them.

FROM RHYTHM TO RHYME

Sing a song of sixpence
A pocket full of rye
Four and twenty blackbirds
Baked in a pie.

When the pie was opened,
The birds began to sing;
Wasn't that a dainty dish
To set before the king?

A gift of song — a gift to please a king. From peasant to cook to king we are all favorably affected by music. It has charms to soothe us, to put us in a good mood, to make us happy or sad. The appropriate strains accompany us to weddings or funerals. It marches us to war. We respond to it instinctively, sometimes by humming along, sometimes by tapping our fingers or feet in time to the rhythm. Audiences have been known to get up and dance in the aisles spontaneously during musicals like *Hair*. For of all the pleasurable features of music, rhythm is the one that exerts the strongest influence on the listener.

Nature is the original source of rhythmic expression. All living things are influenced by the great rhythms of the universe from the turning of the seasons to the movement of the stars. We are so used to these phenomena we are scarcely aware of them as recurring rhythms, scarcely aware of their effect on us as part of the phenomenon.

Our innate delight in rhythmic sound and movement is rooted so far back in evolutionary history it precedes language. For our tribal ancestors, the ritual chants and dances were a natural development growing out of the basic drive for rhythmic expression. Primitive societies that live close to nature still perform such chants and dances, some of which you may have seen and heard on television. Children in our culture preserve the vestiges of ritual incantation in nursery rhymes.

> Rain rain go away
> Come again some other day
> Little Johnny wants to play.

As human beings we are born with a sense of rhythm that, if fostered, continues to develop as we grow. Even before we could walk, we responded to the sound and movement of "pat-a-cake, pat-a-cake, baker's man." From there it was only a step to the longer and slightly more elaborate Mother Goose rhymes. Children love poetry in this form, so much so that many children, my own included, have memorized a whole Mother Goose collection before learning to read.

Unless hopelessly tone-deaf or turned off in grade school by a word-murdering teacher, the adult ear continues to respond favorably to rhythm in poetry and prose. Our conversations are filled with the rhythms of the speaking voice. This last phrase itself has a musical cadence that is lost if we reverse the order of the words to "the speaking voice's rhythms." The awkwardness of the rearranged phrase causes us to avoid it instinctively in the first place and choose the smoother order instead. Unless forced into pretentious wording, everyday speech falls into rhythmic patterns. This again brings up the important bit of advice stressed in Chapter Two: write the way you talk. If you do, your writing will have some natural rhythm.

To understand all the ways rhythm can affect spoken words and therefore written ones would mean studying semantics and acoustics as well as music. Without getting that deeply involved, you can still take advantage of the ear's natural predilection for rhythm by mastering some of the basic devices that preserve and enhance it.

Repetition

We noted previously how an opening sentence or idea, if repeated at the end, can round off a plot quite nicely. One of the reasons it does this is that it satisfies our sense of rhythm. In William Carlos Williams' "The Dance," the repetition in "The dancers go round, they go round and around" adds to the poem's rollicking measure. There are other devices that reinforce the rhythm of the poem also, notably repetitions of consonant and vowel sounds.

Repetition of the initial consonant in two or more words in a phrase or sentence is known as alliteration. Alliteration occurs frequently in nursery rhymes (*S*ing a *s*ong of *s*ixpence) as well as in other kinds of poetry. Williams used it to good advantage in "The Dance" and so did Auden in "Loneliness" with "*g*ate-crashing *g*host" and "*b*lackmailing *b*rute." You don't have to be a poet to appreciate alliteration. It appears in any number of everyday expressions: *l*ive and *l*et *l*ive, *bl*ack and *bl*ue, *h*old your *h*orses, *g*one but not forgotten. The list is endless because new ones continue to crop up all the time, *d*iffuse as spring *d*andelions.

What alliteration accomplishes with consonants, assonance achieves with vowels. You find assonance in these common expressions: d*ow*n and *ou*t, h*i*gh and m*i*ghty, *u*p and c*o*ming. Some familiar sayings like g*o*ne but n*o*t forg*o*tten contain assonance and alliteration both. Another variation of rhythm can be obtained by shifting to a slightly different vowel instead of repeating a previous one. A progression of related but different vowel sounds can give your writing a pleasing variation of sound.

Alliteration has figured prominently in poetry from the time of the earlier epics, but not until this century has it achieved comparable popularity in prose. Possibly due to the influence of James Joyce, who brought it to an unsurpassed peak in Ulysses, we find alliterative phrases in the prose of writers with styles as diverse as John Updike and John Gardner. Read aloud this next paragraph from the novel *Grendel* and listen to the lovely rhythm Gardner creates with various kinds of repetition:

> Talking, talking, spinning a spell, pale skin of words that closes me in like a coffin. Not in a language that anyone any longer understands. Rushing degenerate mutter of noises I send out before me wherever I creep, like a dragon burning his way through vines and fog.

Scanning for Rhythm
Since a good writer has his ear attuned naturally to the musical cadence of a spoken or written line, he doesn't usually have to check consciously for rhythm. He can trust his instinct. If you are a little unsure of this aspect of writing, read your work out loud.

Better still, read it into a tape recorder and play it back for critical listening. This should solve the problem because if there are any clumsy or incompatible places you will hear your voice faltering over them. They should jar your ear like a wrong note struck in a piano solo. However, even if your work does sound off-key, you may not be able to put your finger on the reason. If this is the case, you can scan your lines to determine the predominant rhythm. When you have found that, you can check to see if you have repeated it at appropriate intervals.

Scanning a line means breaking it down into component sections called feet. The composition of language is so closely allied to that of music that any line of prose or poetry can be separated into rhythmic feet containing combinations of weak and heavy stresses very similar to musical measures. The emphasis of your reading voice tells you where the heavy beat is in each foot (Sing/ a song/ of sixpence). There are four standard feet in written English.

Iambic: a light followed by a stressed syllable. The commonest line in English poetry is the iambic pentameter, five feet in a predominant iambic rhythm. (Uneas/y lies/ the head/ that wears/ a crown.) Shakespeare, like other writers before and after him, wrote frequently in iambic pentameter. An ear for rhythm will pick out this basic pattern easily because we hear it every day all around us.

> The Ran/gers will/ be back/ in ac/tion soon./
> I plan/ to trade/ it in/ this fall/ for sure./
> The cost/ of liv/ing rose/ again/ last month./

Trochaic: a stressed syllable followed by a light one. (Mary,/ Mary/ quite con/trary,/ How does your/ garden/ grow?) Trochaic is the reverse of iambic, and like iambic, can be heard frequently in everyday expressions.

> Money/ doesn't/ grow on/ trees, you/ know.
> Fill it/ up and/ check the/ oil, please./
> Must you/ leave so/ soon? It's/ early/ yet.

Dactylic: a stressed syllable followed by two light syllables. (In Breughel's great/ picture, the/ Kermess, the/ dancers go/ round, they go/ round and a/round.) Since this is the waltze time of rhythmic language, it is no accident that Williams chose it for "The dance." You can hear this one, too, in everyday speech.

What in the/ world did I/ do with my/ books?
Where do you/ think you are/ going this/ time of night?
This is the/ best of the/ lot.

Anapestic: two light syllables followed by a stressed syllable. (At the
seige/ of Belleisle/ I was there/ all the while.) Anapestic is the
reverse of dactylic.

When he fin/ally phoned,/she was out.
Do you think/ you can do/ it alone?
So I said/ to her, Ma/ry, I said . . . .

None of the examples above would be spoken quite the way they are
scanned here with the stress falling equally on the marked syllables.
In actual conversation there would be half-note modulations with
varying degrees of emphasis. In "The Rangers will be back in action
soon," the second syllables of "Rangers" and "action" would receive
a slightly heavier emphasis and the word "will" would receive less.

Variation

It is one thing to reinforce rhythm in your writing, but prose or
poetry whose meter (structured rhythm) is perfectly regular will
come across as jingly as a Mother Goose rhyme. *Mary had a little
lamb, its fleece was white as snow* appeals to children because of its
singsong quality. This is fine for the five-year-old, but the adult
palate demands more sophisticated fare. To satisfy the need for
variety, the rhythm-conscious writer varies his patterns. Even free
verse — which isn't really free at all — has recurring feet. What is
wanted in modern prose and poetry is a predominant meter with
plenty of variations.

Prose writers can use a variety of devices to avoid monotony.
Moving subordinate clauses to different positions in the sentences
throughout a paragraph is one way to achieve variation. Another
way is to vary the length of the sentences. In the lovely paragraph we
quoted from John Gardner's *Grendel*, there is one short sentence
between two long ones. The first and third sentences in this section
are pure poetry; the middle sentence, by way of contrast, is short,
prosaic, matter-of-fact. Winston Churchill, one of the great prose
stylists of this century, was well aware of the effect of variations in
sentence lengths. In the wartime speech in which he quoted the
defeatist Petain as saying Hitler would wring the necks of the
English like chickens, Churchill ended with "Some chicken. Some
neck."

"Some neck" is a spondee, a foot containing two heavy beats of equal stress. A spondee can be used for emphasis as in Churchill's speech, or to denote strong emotion as in Macbeth's famous soliloquy spoken after the tortured usurper is told of his wife's death.

> . . . Out, out, brief candle!
> Life's but a walking shadow, a poor player
> That struts and frets his hour upon the stage
> And then is heard no more.

In all there are nineteen kinds of rhythmic feet with a vocabulary to match. The five explained in detail here are the most common. The nomenclature isn't important; it merely serves as a convenient handle for reference purposes. What is important is to apply, consciously or unconcsciously, a suitable rhythm in your writing and if it sounds faulty, to know how to scan it and change it.

Padding

One temptation peculiar to inexperienced poets is the urge to insert totally useless and unnecessary words in a line in order to pad out the meter. *Does*, a silly little supplementary verb form seeming to possess special fascination for rhythmists, is one of the most frequent offenders. Seasoned poets spurn this word just as they do *o'er* and *e'er* and other unnatural contractions. Again, *write the way you talk* and you will be able to resist this kind of padding:

EAGLE

> When to the earth he does descend
> 'tis then his majesty does end.
> I laugh o'er his ungainly stance.
> An eagle's walk is not a dance.

We could improve this at least a little by cutting out the unnecessary words and getting closer to the normal way of speaking.

> He is no king when he descends
> to earth. Then his majesty ends.
> I laugh at his ungainly stance —
> An eagle's walk is no dance.

Matching Sound to Sense

It should be obvious by now that a perfectly regular meter is not what is wanted. The modern ear is so used to a jangling cacophony of sounds that an atonal rhythm or even a harsh one may be more suited to today's tastes. The harmony of the stars is one thing; life in a twentieth-century city is another. If, as some artists maintain, art should reflect the reality of the times, then as writers we can't ignore strife, noise, violence and the other emotional coinages of our age. Some of this appears in the Beetle's recording of "A Day in the Life" where the music becomes a tone-poem for the events depicted. Like music, your writing can echo any motion or emotion. The most obvious matching of sound and sense occurs as onomatopeia where the word actually imitates the sound it represents: hiss, buzz, murmur, tick-tock, snap, crackle, pop.

Rhyme

Like characterization in the novel and action in drama, rhyme in poetry presents a special problem for writers of this particular genre. There are a large number of anthologies on the market, all subtitled *An Introduction to Poetry*, that discuss rhyme schemes along with the different forms of poetry. There is even a dictionary of rhyming words for those who want made-to-order endings. To rhyme or not to rhyme is a question that bothers the audience at poetry readings more than it bothers the poets themselves. You can find examples of both rhymed and unrhymed verse in the work of most major poets.

For rhyming poets, there are a few things to watch for in general. Avoid using familiar end rhymes. There are more subtle forms that get away from regular rhymes — imperfect rhyme, for example, and internal rhyme. Stay away from the obvious moon-June-soon associations, in favor of different rhyme schemes.

> Therefore as strangers
> we cross a new terrain
> rapt explorers
> of an unmapped country.

A rhyme involving three syllables, triple rhyme, should be shunned as it has a nursery rhyme flavor (hickory-dickory-dock) as well as a comic quality. Byron exploited it for just that reason in *Don Juan*, most particularly in the lines in which he satirized intellectual women:

But — oh! ye lords of ladies intellectual
Inform us truly, have they not hen-pecked you all?

Ogden Nash extended the comic range even further through word-distortions with coinages such as "prepocerous" to rhyme with rhinocerous. And that is the main problem with blunt rhyme of any kind: it has comic connotations.

Summary
Rhythm is a natural and intrinsic element of man and his language. Once you become aware of rhythm patterns and how they work, you can use them to advantage in your writing through the application of these few pointers:

- Use normal speech patterns for their natural rhythms.
- Read your work out loud to test the rhythm.
- Scan the lines manually to test the rhythm.
- Increase the rhythm in your writing through alliteration and assonance or through repetition of syllables, words or phrases.
- Avoid obvious rhyme schemes in favor of more subtle forms.

ODDS AND ENDS

Now that you have reached this point in *The Creative Writer's Handbook*, you will, I hope, have spotted some of your own weaknesses and become more aware of ways in which you can improve. When your writing is going well, you are on top of the world. I don't have to tell you it is the most beautiful natural high there is. As one neophyte, an elderly man in his first creative writing class put it, it is like being in inner space. On the other hand, the most frustrating experience for a writer is to go through a dry run or even to feel that there is nothing left to write about. One of the reasons, perhaps, why the suicide rate is rather high among writers. A writer who feels written out may feel he has nothing else worth living for.

Writer's Block

Writer's block is a common condition nearly all writers experience at some time or other. The Pierre Bertons among us who employ research assistants and have filing cabinets full of waiting material can approach the typewriter confident of putting in six to eight hours of productive work daily. But most writers aren't in that category and most have to face times when they sit and stare at an intimidating sheet of white paper and no words come. The front burner is cold. Then they become either depressed or panicky, and the more they worry the worse the block becomes.

The problem of writer's block usually stems from an expectation that all allotted writing time should be spent in the physical activity of putting words on paper. Thus most writers, because their time is limited, demand of themselves a word count for every minute spent in front of the typewriter. This is too rigid an expectation — fallow times are important too if seen and appreciated for what they are. Earlier we mentioned carrying a notebook with you at all times so that you can get your thoughts down right away. What is needed next is thinking time, the "gestation" period between the conception of the idea and the birth of the poem or story. Give the seed time to sprout and put down roots. Instead of trying to pound a thought into quick growth, *sit quietly and do nothing* — just let your mind play with the idea you want to work up. The gestation period can bring rewarding results.

An understanding of how the creative process works can help you get through a writer's block with a minimum of distress. Creativity has been described as 10% inspiration and 90% perspiration. But this definition leaves out the gestation period. The creative process is actually a three-part formula:

1. inspiration
2. gestation
3. perspiration

If you leap into the perspiration stage too fast, you may find yourself doggedly pushing one uninspired word after another. If you are persistent you can force yourself to sit at the typewriter and slog out an allotment of words, so many hundred or thousand a day. Such industriousness may be productive, but of what? The true creative writer wants an end result that justifies the effort put into it. Inspiration, however, works in mysterious ways its wonders to perform. It can occur as an initial "eureka" or it can come in spurts of insight while you are writing. For some writers, pedestrian writing helps to keep them going until the excitement starts up again. One word leads to another, slowly at first, then faster and faster and soon they are off, fingers flying. When it works, this is one way of unblocking.

A different and more frightening kind of writer's block lies not in the gestation or perspiration stages but in the failure to generate ideas. When you haven't jotted down a fresh thought for weeks or even months, you become more than discouraged. You begin to despair of ever writing another word. How do you get started again? Maybe you need a totally new perspective or a new emotional stimulation of some kind, or perhaps just a sharpened alertness to the writing possibilities that exist around you. We live in an amazingly complex world seething with situations crying out for creative interpretation. No one by any stretch of the imagination could write about all of it. Therefore it is nonsense to say that a writer is permanently written out. What has happened is that his enthusiasm has temporarily gone dead. The creative batteries can usually be recharged by one of the following positive-action steps:

ARRANGE FOR A CHANGE OF SCENE

Writers who can afford to travel. A change of scenery opens up new horizons in more ways than one. Even without leaving the country, a change of scene can be experienced by changing jobs, quitting school or going back to school, or adopting a different life style.

UNDERGO A NEW EMOTIONAL EXPERIENCE.

An emotional reaction can't be ordered up like a bottle of strong medicine from the drug store, but when something disturbing happens to you, use it. Losing a loved one, undergoing a separation or divorce, or any similar emotional upheaval, generally brings on renewed creative activity. Not that I'm advocating a divorce to start you writing again, but if something painful does happen, write about it.

READ UP ON SOMETHING TOTALLY DIFFERENT.

If you feel stale, challenge your mental capacities with reading matter chosen from a discipline entirely different from literature. Delve into science, business or politics. Read biographies of leaders in other professions. Read newspaper columnists for insight into current events.

TAKE A COURSE IN SOMETHING

— Anything. If it does nothing else for your writing, a stimulating course will add new words to your vocabulary and new images to your repertoire.

JOIN A CREATIVE WRITERS' CLUB.

If there isn't one in your town or city, start one. You will be surprised at the response you will get from a notice posted on the bulletin board of the public library or inserted in the community-events column of your local paper. A writers' club will put you in contact with others who have concerns similar to yours. There is nothing like a sharing of ideas to get you going again.

CHANGE TO A DIFFERENT MEDIUM FOR AWHILE.

This is my own solution to the problem of writers' block. Poetry is my first love, but the writing of book reviews, magazine articles, prose texts, fiction — all have provided satisfactory substitutes when the poetry won't flow. If I concentrate on prose temporarily, ideas for poems will begin to generate and dam up until one day the dam breaks and I'm off again.

None of these suggestions is infallible. Most of them probably are not practical or even possible in your particular case. But if even one works for you — well, one is all it takes to break the block.

Props and Preparations

Writer's block is not the only problem faced by writers. Sometimes even an experienced writer with plenty to say will have trouble with the first words. This is when a writer's prop is helpful. A favorite cup full of fresh coffee, a special pen or some similar object can help trigger the actual beginning. A prop is fine as long as it doesn't become so important that if you lose it you are lost yourself.

How do you begin? Put anything down. You can always go back and change it. Margaret Laurence says she made at least three different starts on *The Fire Dwellers*. Finally put it aside, wrote *A Jest of God*, then went back to *The Fire Dwellers*. You can put an entire work aside temporarily or you can work on other sections of it until, somewhere along the line, a beginning suggests itself.

All artists, writers included, can get so wrapped up in a piece of work that they cannot see it objectively. A painter can hold his painting upside down or up to a mirror to get a fresh view of it. Doris Lessing's neighbor used to get up in the middle of the night and rush into his studio to look at the painting he'd been working on that afternoon. Try reading your work over at a different time of day. If you know a published author, ask that person to read part of your manuscript. Better still, especially if it is poetry you write, send a sample to the editor of one of the little magazines and ask for constructive criticism. And then try to see your poem through these disinterested eyes.

Style

Another problem, one that bothers beginning writers unnecessarily, is style. In the first place, what does the term really mean? If we say a certain person has style, we are speaking of more than dress. Flair and imagination in the way clothes are worn lend distinction to the wearer. Similarly, in writing, the words chosen and they way they are put together give a writer his individual style. This invariably reflects everything put into the work. Your style is the sum total of everything you are. You don't have to strive to achieve it. Furthermore, style has to be fluid and capable of change. Writers need to be chameleons so that they can psyche themselves into different roles much the way actors do. When a writer's themes change, a corresponding change of style usually suggests itself.

If, in spite of these remarks, you still want to work at developing a distinctive style, go ahead and experiment. Try new ideas. But don't ignore established methods. A theme may require one or the other or both. Remember the new has no meaning without the old. If you align yourself exclusively on the side of innovation, you will cut yourself off from the common literary heritage. On the other hand, if you stick with the safe and accepted styles of the past you may become a victim of hardening of the creative arteries. In severe cases this results in the death of the imagination. A good writer knows he needs both experimental and established forms because both are part of his own intellectual and emotional being. Your style will reflect the stage of maturity you have achieved.

Don't rush it. Have something to say and say it well. Shakespeare worked within the accepted traditions of his time. Even Picasso went through a number of traditional stages before his later and distinctive style established itself. Be what you are, express what you feel as honestly as you can, and style will take care of itself.

Rewriting

Some advice about rewriting is in order next. This is the stage where much of the perspiration occurs. Going over a work to put it in final shape, knocking out the rouch places, checking and rechecking — all this is hard work. It is also very gratifying to the true craftsman to see his story or poem acquiring its final polish. For some writers there is a sensual pleasure in adding the final touches. At any rate, the craftsmanship necessary to rework the material, if not as exciting as its conception, brings an added glow of accomplishment. Farley Mowat says that for him the satisfaction that comes from writing lies above all in being a good practitioner, a good capable craftsman. It is an enduring satisfaction.

Writers who complain they don't like to go over their work and revise because it spoils the freshness are suffering from a dangerous delusion. Only a blind egoist thinks every word of his so precious not one can be changed. Writers concerned with the best possible product rewrite constantly. Sometimes a writer finds it necessary to change whole sections as well as words or lines. Mordecai Richler rewrote some chapters intended for *St. Urbaine's Horseman* ten or fifteen times — and then took them out altogether. He says that no matter how dazzling those places were, they were there at the expense of the whole novel. So out they came.

What do you look for when rewriting? Adopt a regular pattern of checks. Look at the big things first. Are theme, tone and characterization consistent within themselves and comfortable with each other? Do symbols and images point like signposts to an overall meaning? Is the ending strong, or if ambiguous, did you intend it to be so? Can your poem or story be tightened up? There are probably repetitious places that could be eliminated. Next, examine the details. Have you been explicit enough? Have you given the reader enough details necessary for a clear picture? On the other hand, have you used too many details, too many adjectives, too many wordy descriptions? Can your diction be improved in places with a stronger or more appropriate word? Have you provided for variety? Have you left something for the reader's imagination?

Finally you should go over the whole thing for grammar and spelling. For a long prose work like a play or a novel, this is time-consuming but not difficult. You can do it yourself. However, if you are unsure of grammar rules, ask an English teacher to read your manuscript. If you don't know any English teachers, ask the principal of your neighborhood school to recommend one, perhaps one who is retired.

After you have gone over your work for grammar and spelling, put it aside for a few days and *don't look at it during this resting period.* Do something entirely different in the meantime — clean the apartment, read a novel, start writing something else. When you go back to what you thought was a finished work, you will be amazed at the ragged places that will jump out at you. Only after you have gone over the entire thing again until every inconsistency and error has been remedied will you be ready to send it to a publisher.

What do editors look for in a manuscript? As one of the editors of *Mainline*, a little poetry magazine that flourished in the 60's and early 70's, I know what caught and held my attention: something a little different from the hundreds of other submissions received. I looked for evidence of love of language, imaginative imagery, a fresh stimulating idea or an original approach to an old one — in short, any and all of the points covered in the preceding chapters of this handbook.

Conclusion

Writing is a very demanding occupation and one of the loneliest. But for the dedicated writer, no other activity in the whole universe can compare with it. It is an occupation that will sustain you for the rest of your life. Unlike arts that demand physical exertion, you can expect your writing powers to increase, not decline, as you grow older. Yeats wrote his best poetry in his early seventies. If you believe in your writing self and maintain your enthusiasm, somewhere along the line you are going to climb over the fence that separates the dabbler from the serious writer. I hope this handbook has made you a little more aware of the tools that will get you there.

May your writing go as you want it to.

ACKNOWLEDGEMENTS

John Gardner, "Talking talking, spinning a spell...," from *Grendel*. © 1971 by John Gardner. Reprinted by permission of Alfred A. Knopf, Inc.

Faye Kicknosway, "Return Postage," © 1974 by Faye Kicknosway. Reprinted from *A Man is a Hook. Trouble.* by permission of Capra Press.

C.H. Molloy, "The World is Late," reprinted with the kind permission of the poet.

Pablo Neruda, "Sonata: There's No Forgetting," from *Spanish-American Literature in Translation*, Willis Knapp Jones, Ed. © 1963 by Frederick Ungar Publishing Co., Inc.

Linda Renwick, "Moments Like These," reprinted with the kind permission of the poet.

Josephine Hambleton Tessier, "From Millhaven," reprinted with the kind permission of the poet.

Eve Tihanyi, "This Room," from the collection entitled *The Chameleon Confesses*, reprinted with the kind permission of the poet.